Human Trafficking as a New (In)Security Threat

Elżbieta M. Goździak

Human Trafficking as a New (In)Security Threat

palgrave
macmillan

Elżbieta M. Goździak
Center for Migration Studies
Adam Mickiewicz University
Poznań, Poland

ISBN 978-3-030-62872-7 ISBN 978-3-030-62873-4 (eBook)
https://doi.org/10.1007/978-3-030-62873-4

Cover illustration: Brain light/Alamy Stock Photo

This Palgrave Macmillan imprint is published by the registered company Springer Nature Switzerland AG
The registered company address is: Gewerbestrasse 11, 6330 Cham, Switzerland

Contents

CHAPTER 1

Introduction

On January 8, 2019, Donald J. Trump, speaking from the Oval Office in the White House, warned the American people that if a wall is not erected along the Mexican border, drugs, criminals, and terrorists will continue pouring into the country and will jeopardize the national security of the United States. Fact-checkers quickly reminded Mr. Trump that according to the US State Department, "there was no credible evidence indicating that international terrorist groups have established bases in Mexico, worked with Mexican drug cartels, or sent operatives via Mexico into the United States" (DOS 2018: 205). Moreover, data from the US Department of Homeland Security (DHS) indicate that most individuals on the terrorist watch list attempted to enter the United States by air. Most of the 2,554 people on the terrorist watch list who were encountered by US officials in 2017 tried to enter through airports (2,170) or by sea (49) (DHS 2018: 9). I am sure these facts will not prevent Donald Trump from continuing to argue that traffickers bring terrorists and drugs across the southern border.

Donald Trump is not the first US president that has connected human trafficking, a crime not normally associated with national security, with the need to protect the nation (see Stinson 2012). In the aftermath of the terrorist attacks on the United States on 9/11, President George W. Bush identified the correlation as more than a mere theoretical

E. M. Goździak, *Human Trafficking as a New (In)Security Threat*,
https://doi.org/10.1007/978-3-030-62873-4_1

concern by signing on December 16, 2002, 70th National Security Directive 22, which specifically linked human trafficking to terrorist threats. Two years later, the US Congress passed the Intelligence Reform and Terrorism Prevention Act of 2004, which established the Human Smuggling and Trafficking Center, composed of experts from the prosecutorial, law enforcement, consular, policy, intelligence, and diplomatic areas, to study the nexus of human trafficking and smuggling and the criminal support of underground terrorist travel (Intelligence Reform and Terrorism Prevention Act 2004). Additionally, the Trafficking Victims Protection Reauthorization Act (TVPRA) of 2005 created an interagency task force with a mandate to explore the "interrelationships between trafficking in persons and terrorism" (Rizer and Glaser 2011: 70).

Donald J. Trump and George W. Bush are also not the only world leaders who claimed that human trafficking—often conflated with irregular migration—is a security threat. Viktor Orbán, the Prime Minister of Hungary, used the same argument to reject refugees fleeing conflicts in the Middle East and build his own Fortress Hungary. Jarosław Kaczyński, the current leader of the Peace and Justice Party (PiS) in Poland, also linked migration with insecurity and a threat to 'Christian Europe' (Leszczyński 2017). The list of politicians presenting similar arguments is long.

Indeed, the framing of human trafficking as a security threat constitutes a part of a much broader attempt to portray migration across international borders as a security risk. Once it was announced that the 19 hijackers, who attacked the Twin Towers in New York City, the Pentagon in Washington, DC, and crashed a plane in Shanksville, Pennsylvania, were foreign nationals, those critical of the US immigration system argued that the government must use all available means to protect the country's national security. The critics called for "enhancing and enlarging the border security functions of the Immigration and Naturalization Service (INS)" (Chebel d'Appolonia 2012: 1). Within a few days, the Immigration and Nationality Act was adopted and a series of reforms aimed at implementing immigration restrictions, including the detention of foreign-born individuals without charge, began.

Terrorist attacks in Paris, Brussels, and Nice have sparked similar assertions in Europe, despite the fact that the terrorists were French and Belgian citizens. Facts notwithstanding, policy-makers on both sides of the Atlantic allege that human smuggling and human trafficking are a conduit for international terrorism. On September 20, 2001, the Council of the European Union called for the strengthening of surveillance measures, including vigilance in issuing residency permits and systematic checking of identity papers, under Article 2.3 of the Schengen Convention. The bombings in Madrid on March 11, 2004, and London on July 7, 2005, further consolidated the national security policies in Europe.

Anti-refugee and anti-immigrant sentiments in the United States and in many European countries stem from the perception that "migrants pose a socio-economic and ethno-cultural threat to western societies" (Chebel d'Appolonia 2012: 13). In the United States, the sitting president considers El Salvador, Haiti, and myriad African states "shithole countries" (Woodhouse 2018). He has banned travel from several Muslim-majority countries and the Supreme Court, in a ruling 5-4, upheld the ban (Siddiqui 2018). Trump also said that immigrants in the country illegally are responsible for tens of thousands of crimes (Horsley 2018), although his former Chief of Staff, John Kelly, in an interview with the National Public Radio (NPR), acknowledged that most people crossing the border illegally do not pose a security threat (Burnett and Gonzales 2018).

Immigrants are also regarded as threatening national identity and social cohesion. The current 'refugee crisis' in Europe has resulted in public discussions about the threat that Muslim refugees pose to the Christian identity of the continent. The debates are especially fervent in the new accession countries in Central Europe (Goździak and Márton 2018).

However, these anti-immigrant sentiments and conceptualizations of migrants as criminals and terrorists and irregular migration as trafficking predate the terrorist attacks by at least a decade or more. In the 1990s, conservative discourses identified multiculturalism as a cause of societal disintegration. The best-known version of this kind of discourse is Huntington's *The Clash of Civilizations* (1996). It mediates the differentiation between us and them by identifying other peoples and cultures that endanger the survival of the home culture. Migration is identified as being one of the main elements weakening national tradition and threatening societal homogeneity.

Throughout this book, the readers will see discussions of instances where the nexus of human trafficking and security has been emphasized much more strongly than is perhaps warranted. We will also see how the concept of human trafficking is being stretched—by policymakers, the media, and researchers—almost to the point of losing its meaning. Concerns of national security overshadowed the original focus on exploited labor, sexual exploitation, and human insecurity of trafficked persons, refugees, and migrants. However, before I introduce the reader to what lies ahead, let me discuss my own positionality vis-à-vis the topics explored in this book.

Researching Human Trafficking

I have been researching human trafficking for almost two decades. I started shortly after the passage, in 2000, of the Protocol to Prevent, Suppress, and Punish Trafficking in Persons, Especially Women and Children, supplementing the United Nations Convention against Organized Crime, and the subsequent US legislation, the Trafficking Victims Protection Act (TVPA).

First, I mainly studied up—decision-makers, policies, and programs set up to prevent human trafficking, protect survivors, and prosecute perpetrators—because access to trafficked victims, guarded by their traffickers, and survivors, watched over equally fervidly by service providers, was impossible and research funds scarce. Most of the money appropriated by the US Congress for anti-trafficking activities was spent on awareness-raising campaigns or direct services to victims. International resources were also very limited. Later on, as I gained trust of service providers, I was slowly able to meet a few survivors of trafficking and was able to study down, analyzing the meaning survivors ascribe to their trafficking experiences, and identifying the strategies they employ to build their lives in the destination countries or upon return to countries of origin. I also studied sideways, comparing the experiences of various survivors and assistance approaches in different countries. I researched children trafficked to the United States, adolescents forced to smuggle people and drugs across the US-Mexico border, laboring children at risk for trafficking in Nepal and Cambodia, adult victims trafficked to the United States as well as adults trafficked to Western Europe, Russia, and the Middle East who returned home to Poland, Moldova, Nepal, and Thailand. I also studied refugees seeking safe haven in Hungary and turned away because of fear of terrorists hiding among them. I explored discourses deployed in the Visegrád countries of Poland, Hungary, Slovakia, and the Czech Republic that conceptualize those aiding refugees fleeing Syria, Iraq, and Afghanistan as human traffickers.

As a scholar of international migration, I have focused on mobility across international borders. Therefore, my research on human trafficking has almost exclusively centered on cross-border trafficking. I published one essay about how the rhetorical and policy shift in the United States toward domestic youth in forced prostitution has affected the broader efforts to fight trafficking of foreign nationals both in the sex and other industries, but this was a singular foray into the realm of domestic trafficking (Goździak 2020). As an anthropologist, I have strived to depart from the 'master narrative' (Snajdr 2013) presenting innocent victims held captive by evil traffickers or rescued by Good Samaritans. I have also rejected the master narrative portraying service providers as one-dimensional abolitionists. Instead, I continue to deploy an ethnographic approach focused on getting the insiders' view of their experiences—whether these experiences involve being smuggled by a *coyote* or being exploited by unscrupulous employers. I try to elicit a range of views from stakeholders as well.

Similar to other anthropological studies of mobility and mobile populations, most of my research on human trafficking takes the form of *unsited (or mobile) field* (Cook et al. 2009). Although I often spend weeks or months on any given study, few of the interviews I conduct stem from 'accidental encounters' or 'chance events' (MacClancey 2002). I mostly rely on the scheduled 'interview moment.' There are no communities of survivors of human trafficking. Most live among other immigrants or local people and no amount of 'deep hanging out' (Geertz 1998) will result in easy identification of survivors of human trafficking. In order to gain access to them, I had to rely on close collaboration with service providers. Similarly, a visit to a refugee camp requires permissions from a variety of gatekeepers. Without their approval, I am not able to proceed.

While unable to spend more than a couple of hours with each survivor, service provider, or policy-maker, I nevertheless conceptualize my research as an ethnographic endeavor. I travel to 'the field' to observe programs in action, participate in or organize working meetings with a variety of caseworkers, attorneys, and law enforcement representatives working with survivors, conduct focused group discussions and individual in-depth interviews with program staff, and interview survivors in their place of residence, at their worksites, and at the programs where they are being served. This on-site research is quite different from the approach used by law enforcement, attorneys, and, to some extent, social workers who are mainly interested in facts. They often do not consider the context that frames the survivors' experiences and do not analyze the situation from the survivors' point of view. Their objective is to fit the information obtained from survivors into predetermined legal or assistance frameworks.

In contrast, my aim has always been to listen to the trafficked individuals as well as stakeholders to present their points of view in order to understand how survivors conceptualize their trafficking experiences and their traffickers, what they perceive to be their most urgent needs, and how these perceptions might differ from the conceptualizations and approaches of the service providers. I also want to understand how stakeholders and anti-trafficking advocates see the phenomenon of human trafficking and its links to security issues. I want to elicit *their* stories whether the stories come from interviews or from close reading of documents and discourses.

Writing About Human Trafficking

I have written extensively about human trafficking. My publications include reviews and assessments of literature on human trafficking (see Laczko and Goździak 2005; Goździak and Collett 2005; Goździak 2015) and publications based on my own empirical research (See Goździak and MacDonnel 2007; Goździak 2014; Goździak 2016a, b).

In review articles, I have taken issue with the lack of publications based on rigorous empirical research, unknown samples, and scarcity of accounts presenting survivors' points of view. As Denise Brennan writes: "Many authors find themselves writing on an issue that has been sensationalized, misrepresented, and politicized" (Brennan 2005: 36), but few acknowledge this situation and even fewer try to remedy it (Agustín 2007). With some exceptions (e.g., Mahdavi 2001; Zhang 2012; Brennan 2014), most writings focus on trafficking for sexual exploitation of women and girls. Much of the publications on women trafficked for sexual exploitation present them as lacking agency. As Weitzer (2007: 452) points out "the denial of agency is evident in the very framing of the problem as one involving 'prostituted women,' 'trafficking,' and 'sexual slavery.'" Many writers deem the notion of consent irrelevant when it comes to sex trafficking. Ironically, women and men trafficked for other forms of labor exploitation are often considered to be smuggled on the basis that they consented to being taken across international borders. I have also argued that the focus on trauma and vulnerability without recognition of resiliency presents trafficked individuals as helpless and hopeless, beaten and sexually abused victims (Goździak 2014). This 'perfect victim' paradigm prevalent in contemporary discourse denies "gendered victims any sort of agency or voice" (Warren 2012: 109).

In my publications based on empirical research with trafficking survivors, I analyzed the coexistence of agency and vulnerability, and the interplay of trauma and resiliency in survivors of human trafficking. In my book, *Trafficked Children and Youth in the United States. Reimagining Survivors* (Goździak 2016a), I juxtaposed programmatic responses—based on the 'best interest of the child'—with the young survivors' perceptions of their experiences and service needs. I explored the tension between the adolescents' narratives of their trafficking and the actions and discourses of the foster care and child welfare programs. The former are grounded in culturally diverse conceptualizations of childhoods, and the latter are based on Western, middle-class ideals of childhood, which inform programmatic responses toward trafficked minors.

Considering Security

With regard to security, I have explored different facets of human (in)security as narrated by survivors of human trafficking for sexual exploitation and other forms of labor. In my previous publications, I was particularly attentive to the insecurity of trafficking survivors' livelihoods and their tenuous prospects for long-term economic self-sufficiency. On occasion, I also paid attention to personal security of survivors of trafficking. Many service providers worry about physical safety of survivors, especially youth, and take considerable precautions to do everything possible to not put young survivors at risk for re-trafficking.

In this book, I take a broader perspective on security. In today's globalized and transnational world, it is more and more difficult to produce clear-cut taxonomies of security concerns. I look at security on a continuum—from global, national/regional to human (in)security—and analyze the confluence of human trafficking, illegal migration, drug trafficking, terrorism, and organized crime. The analysis is foregrounded in a combination of ethnography, discourse analysis, and policy review. My ethnographic data come from research with survivors of human trafficking, both adults and adolescents, service providers, advocates, and policy-makers in the United States and in Europe. I analyze discourses found in popular media outlets, including social media, and analyze policies pertaining to human trafficking, labor migration, and forced migration.

The Chapters Ahead

Human Trafficking as a New (In)Security Threat challenges the popular rhetoric linking 'war on terror' with 'war on human trafficking' by juxtaposing lived experiences of survivors of trafficking, refugees, and labor migrants with macro-level security concerns. The book is divided into three distinct parts. In Part One, I present the historical antecedents and contemporary manifestations of human trafficking and its links to national security. In Part Two, I focus on the Other—refugees and asylum seekers—perceived as a national security threat. I spotlight the US refugee resettlement program—its history, slow erosion, and the current danger of possible elimination—and argue that a robust refugee resettlement is not a threat but an asset to our national security. In the following chapter, I focus on Hungary and Poland to showcase how human trafficking has replaced or been conflated with migration in public narratives, policy responses, and practice with refugees. In Part Three, I analyze lived experiences of (in)security of trafficked victims, irregular migrants, and asylum seekers in the United States and in Europe, with a special focus on unaccompanied children and adolescents.

In the concluding chapter, I try to answer the question of how security concerns stemming from human trafficking can be reconciled with the need to protect victims.

References

Agustín, Laura. 2007. *Sex at the Margins. Migration, Labour Markets and the Rescue Industry*. London: Zed Books.

Brennan, Denise. 2005. Methodological Challenges in Research with Trafficked Persons: Tales from the Field. *International Migration* 43 (1/2): 35–54. https://doi.org/10.1111/j.0020-7985.2005.00311.x.

Brennan, Denise. 2014. *Life Interrupted: Trafficking into Forced Labor in the United States*. Durham, NC: Duke University Press.

Burnett, John and Richard Gonzales. 2018. John Kelly on Trump, the Russia Investigation and Separating Immigrant Families. *NPR*, May 10. Audio https://www.npr.org/2018/05/10/609478998/john-kelly-despite-times-of-deep-frustration-no-regrets-taking-white-house-job.

Chebel d'Appollonia, Ariane. 2012. *Frontiers of Fear. Immigration and Insecurity in the United States and Europe*. Ithaca: Cornell University Press.

Cook, Joanna, James Laidlwa, and Johnathan Mair. 2009. What If There Is No Elephant? Towards Conception of an Un-Sited Field. In *Multi-Sited Ethnography: Theory, Praxis and Locality in Contemporary Research*, ed. M-A Falzon, 73–85. Farnham: Ashgate.

Department of Homeland Security. 2018. *DOJ, DHS Report: Three Out of Four Individuals Convicted of International Terrorism and Terrorism-Related Offenses were Foreign-Born*. Press Release.

Geertz, Clifford. 1998. Deep Hanging Out. *The New York Review of Books*, October 22.

Goździak. 2015. Data Matters: Issues and Challenges for Research on Trafficking. In *Global Human Trafficking. Critical Issues and Contexts*, ed. Molly Dragiewicz, 23–39. Abington: Routledge.

Goździak, Elżbieta M. 2014. Empirical Vacuum: In Search of Research on Human Trafficking. In *The Oxford Handbook on Sex, Gender, and Crime*, eds. Rosemary Gartner and William McCarthy. Oxford: Oxford University Press.

Goździak, Elżbieta M. 2016a. *Trafficked Children and Youth in the United States. Reimagining Survivors*. New Brunswick, NJ: Rutgers University Press.

Goździak, Elżbieta M. 2016b. Of Will or Force? Contesting Assumptions about Child Trafficking. In *Contested Childhoods: Growing Up in Migrancy*, eds. Marie Louise Seeberg and Elzbieta M. Gozdziak. New York: Springer.

Goździak, Elżbieta M. 2020. Low Hanging Fruit: How Domestic Minor Sex Trafficking Erased Foreign-born Victims of Child Trafficking from Anti-trafficking Efforts in the United States. *Journal of Human Trafficking* 6 (2): 226–233. https://doi.org/10.1080/23322705.2020.1691821.

Goździak, Elżbieta M., and Elizabeth A. Collett. 2005. Research on Human Trafficking in North America: A Review of Literature. *International Migration* 43 (1/2): 99–128. https://doi.org/10.1111/j.0020-7985.2005.00314.x.

Goździak, Elżbieta M., and Margaret MacDonnell. 2007. Closing the Gaps: The Need to Improve Identification and Services to Child Victims of Trafficking. *Human Organization Summer* 66 (2): 171–184. https://doi.org/10.17730/humo.66.2.y767h78360721702.

Goździak, Elżbieta M., and Péter Márton. 2018. Where the Wild Things Are: Fear of Islam and the Anti-Refugee Rhetoric in Hungary and in Poland. *Central and Eastern European Migration Review* 7 (2): 125–151. https://doi.org/10.17467/ceemr.2018.04.

Horsley, Scott. 2018. FACT CHECK: Trump, Illegal Immigration, and Crime. Available at https://www.npr.org/2018/06/22/622540331/fact-check-trump-illegal-immigration-and-crime?t=1530190696085.

Huntingtin, Samuel P. 1996. *The Clash of Civilizations*. New York: Touchstone.

Intelligence Reform and Terrorism Prevention Act. 2004. *Title I of Public Law* 118, 108–458, Stat 3688. Washington, DC.

Laczko, Frank and Elżbieta M.Goździak (eds.). 2005. *Data and Research on Human Trafficking: A Global Survey*. Special issue, *International Migration* 43 (1/2).

Leszczyński, Adam. 2017. Piętrowa bzdura Kaczyńskiego o uchodźcach i cywilizacji opartej na chrześcijaństwie. Available at https://oko.press/pietrowa-bzdura-kaczynskiego-o-uchodzcach-cywilizacji-opartej-chrzescijanstwie/.

MacClancey, Jeremy. 2002. *Exotic No More: Anthropology on the Front Lines*. Chicago: Chicago University Press.

Mahdavi, Pardis. 2001. *Gridlock: Labor, Migration, and Human Trafficking in Dubai*. Stanford, CA: Stanford University Press.

Rizer Arthur and Glaser Sheri. 2011. Breach: The National Security Implications of Human Trafficking. *17 Widner Law Review* 69: 76–77.

Siddiqui, Sabrina. 2018. Trump's Travel Ban: What Does the Supreme Court Ruling Mean? *The Guardian*, June 27. Available at https://www.theguardian.com/us-news/2018/jun/26/trump-travel-ban-supreme-court-ruling-explained. Accessed June 28, 2018.

Snajdr, Edward. 2013. Beneath the Master Narrative: Human Trafficking, Myths of Sexual Slavery and Ethnographic Realities. *Dialectical Anthropology* 37: 229–256. https://doi.org/10.1007/s10624-013-9292-3.

Stinson, Ainsley. 2012. *The Securitization of Sex Trafficking: A Comparative Case Study of Sweden and the United States*. B.A.H. (Sociology and International Development) Thesis, Dalhousie University.

US Department of State. 2018. Country Reports on Terrorism 2018. Washington, DC: Mexico.

Weitzer, Ronald. 2007. The Social Construction of Sex Trafficking: Ideology and Institutionalization of a Moral Crusade. *Politics Society* 35: 447–475. https://doi.org/10.1177/0032329207304319.

Warren, Kay B. 2012. Troubling the Victim/Trafficker Dichotomy in Efforts to Combat Human Trafficking: The Unintended Consequences of Moralizing Labor Migration. *Indiana Journal of Global Legal Studies* 19: 105–20. https://doi.org/10.1353/gls.2012.0009.

Woodhouse, Leighton Akio. 2018. Trump's "Shithole Countries" Remark Is at the Center of a Lawsuit to Reinstate Protections for Immigrants. Available at https://theintercept.com/2018/06/28/trump-tps-shithole-countries-lawsuit/.

Zhang, Sheldon X. 2012. *Looking for a Hidden Population: Trafficking of Migrant Laborers in San Diego County*. Washington, DC: National Institute of Justice.

PART I

Understanding Security and Human Trafficking in the 21st Century

What is security? What is human trafficking? Defining these two terms is more than an academic exercise. Terminology matters. It matters to policy, to process, to the law, and to the social and cultural dimensions of both phenomena. Yet, the answers to these questions are not simple. A whole discipline—security studies—has been devoted to answering the first question. But not very successfully, I might add. The definition of security continues to be contested.

Many definitions of human trafficking circulated, with much confusion as to what the term meant, before December 2003 when the United Nations Convention against Transnational Organized Crime and its Protocol on trafficking in persons, known as the *Palermo Protocol*, entered into force. The conceptualization of human trafficking as a security issue accounts for a very high number of countries which became parties to the Protocol. As of 2017, only 20 countries have not signed the Palermo Protocol. Additionally, most countries have passed national anti-trafficking legislations.

Security and human trafficking are concepts that encompass many different dimensions and continue to be expanded. 'Human trafficking' is being stretched—by policy-makers, the media, and researchers–almost to the point of losing its original focus on exploitation for various types of labor, including sexual exploitation. The chapters in this section set the stage for understanding both the historical antecedents and contemporary manifestations of human trafficking (Chapter 2) and the nexus of human trafficking and security (Chapter 3) on the security continuum linking human trafficking, terrorism, organized crime, and irregular migration.

CHAPTER 2

Human Trafficking: Old Phenomenon, New Meaning(s)

Much has been written about the phenomenon of human trafficking. Legal analyses of different international conventions and national laws regarding trafficking in persons abound (see selected bibliographies Goździak 2015; Goździak and Bump 2008). The definition of human trafficking has also been examined (e.g., Plant 2005; Ollus 2015). I, too, have written about human trafficking and included in my publications discussions of the UN Protocol to Prevent, Suppress, and Punish Trafficking in Persons, Especially Women and Children and the US Trafficking Victims Protection Act (TVPA). At the risk of repeating myself, I find it necessary to write again about the historical antecedents that led to the current conceptualization and definition of human trafficking, with a particular focus on the nexus of human trafficking and security (to be addressed in more detail in the following chapter).

The Old and New Abolitionists

The origins of contemporary conceptualizations and debates about human trafficking date back to the end of the nineteenth century when feminists such as Josephine Butler brought involuntary prostitution into the international discourse under the term 'White Slave Trade,' a term derived from the French 'Traite des Blanches,' which was related to 'Traite des Noirs,' a term used in the beginning of the nineteenth century

E. M. Goździak, *Human Trafficking as a New (In)Security Threat*,
https://doi.org/10.1007/978-3-030-62873-4_2

to describe the black slave trade (Derks 2000). "White Slavery" referred to the abduction and transport of white women for prostitution. "For long years past the slaughter of the innocents has been going on," Josephine Butler wrote to her sister in 1898 about international child prostitution. "We knew it not, or only had a partial knowledge of it. Now we know, and before God we are responsible for that terrible knowledge" (Butler 1989: 384). In a manner similar to today's anti-trafficking campaigns, the issue was covered widely in the media, numerous organizations were set up to combat it, and national and international legislation was adopted to stop the trade (Doezema 2002). The nineteenth-century movement against "white slavery" grew out of the campaign in England and other Western European countries; this movement opposed legalization of prostitution and aimed to abolish the practice (Bullough and Bullogh 1987).

In the United States, the 'white slave hysteria' assumed that large numbers of American women were at risk for kidnapping and forced prostitution at the hands of foreign criminals. There are no reliable data to support this claim (Doezema 1999). Scholars suggest that migration of women in order to work as prostitutes has created—in the past and today—a 'moral panic' resulting in the myth of 'white slavery' (Doezema 1999). 'White slavery' has served as a tool for abolitionists to take away the ability of women to choose sex work, and thus restore the 'moral order' of society (Bernstein 2007). The social anxieties and moral indignation about the abuse of innocent women in the 'white slave trade' were an important precursor to contemporary trafficking debates (Lee 2011; see also Woodiwiss and Hobbs 2008).

The first international agreement against 'white slavery' was drafted in 1902 in Paris and signed two years later by sixteen states (Doezema 2002). The International Agreement for the Suppression of the White Slave Trade did not equate 'white slavery' with prostitution. Initially, the agreement addressed the fraudulent or abusive recruitment of women for prostitution in another country; however, in 1910, its scope was broadened to include the trafficking of women and girls within national borders (Wijers and Lap-Chew 1997). In 1921, during a meeting held under the auspices of the League of Nations (later to become the United Nations), the trafficking of boys was also incorporated into the agreement. In 1910, the United States passed the Mann Act, known as the White Slavery Act (18 US Code 2421 Public law 114-38), to address criminal activities and offenses, including prostitution and child pornography.

In 1933, yet another convention was signed in Geneva. The International Convention for the Suppression of the Traffic in Women condemned all recruitment for prostitution in another country. The abolitionist standards of the 1933 Convention were reiterated in the 1949 UN Convention for the Suppression of Traffic in Persons and the Exploitation of the Prostitution of Others, which stated: "Prostitution and the accompanying evil of the traffic in persons for the purpose of prostitution are incompatible with the dignity and worth of a human person and endanger the welfare of the individual, the family, and the community of a person." The 1949 Convention "set standards for the next decades despite the fact that many states did not ratify it, partly because of its abolitionist intent" (Outshoorn 2015: 9).

Trafficking faded from the public eye and prostitution ceased to be a prominent political issue until the 1980s, when a renewed interest in human trafficking was incited by developments regarding migration flows, the feminist movement, the AIDS pandemic, child prostitution, and child sex tourism (Doezema 2002). While women of color, mainly from Southeast Asia and later from Latin America, the Caribbean, and West Africa, were trafficked to Western Europe, it wasn't until white women from Eastern Europe and the former Soviet Union appeared on Europe's doorsteps that human trafficking again captured public imagination. Berman (2003) argues that despite the diversity—racial and ethnic—of trafficked women, the world media and the public discourse presented white women as the primary targets of traffickers. In her book *The Purity Myth*, Valenti (2010) explains that in American culture, the terms 'pure' and 'innocent' have solely been applied to white women. Therefore, they are the only victims worthy of sympathy (Meshkovska and Siegel 2015). I will return to the issue of 'deserving and undeserving victims' later in this book.

Renewed Interest in Human Trafficking at the United Nations

In the 1990s, trafficking in human beings, particularly women and children, reappeared on the agenda of the UN General Assembly, the Commission for Human Rights, the World Conference on Human Rights in Vienna in 1993, and the World Conference on Women in Beijing in 1995. By 1996, seventy countries had ratified the 1949 Convention (Kelly and Regan 2000).

Anne Gallagher (2001) credits Argentina with spearheading the renewed interest in trafficking in persons. Argentina had been interested in the issue of trafficking in minors for a number of years, but was dissatisfied with the slow progress in negotiating an additional protocol to the Convention on the Rights of the Child (CRC) to address child prostitution and child pornography. Although Argentina recognized the human rights dimension of the trafficking phenomenon, it thought it to be insufficient and lobbied strongly for human trafficking to be dealt with as part of the broader international focus on transnational organized crime (Vlassis, cited in Gallagher 2001). Argentina's proposal for a new convention against trafficking in minors was discussed at the 1997 session of the UN Commission on Crime Prevention and Criminal Justice.

In November 2000, the UN General Assembly adopted the UN Protocol to Prevent, Suppress, and Punish Trafficking in Persons, Especially Women and Children, also known as the Palermo Protocol. Other relevant international instruments followed, including the International Labor Organization's Convention Concerning the Prohibition and Immediate Action for the Elimination of the Worst Forms of Child Labor and the Protocol to the Convention on the Right of the Child on the Sale of Children, Child Prostitution and Child Pornography.

The Palermo Protocol was a result of two years of negotiations at the UN Center for International Crime Prevention in Vienna. The Protocol was the target of heavy lobbying efforts by religious and feminist organizations, on the one hand, and human rights advocates, on the other hand. These two groups of activists represented two opposing views of prostitution. The Human Rights Caucus saw prostitution as legitimate labor, while the Coalition Against Trafficking in Women (CATW), representing religious and feminist activists, saw all prostitution as a violation of women's human rights (Doezema 2005). The CATW argued that trafficking should include all forms of recruitment and transportation for prostitution, regardless of whether force or deception took place (Goldscheider 2000). Meanwhile, the Human Rights Caucus, which supported the view of consensual prostitution as work, argued that force or deception was a necessary ingredient in the definition of human trafficking. The Caucus also maintained that the term 'human trafficking' should include trafficking of women, men, and children for different types of labor, including forced sweatshop labor, agriculture, and prostitution. The Global Alliance Against Traffic in Women (GAATW), founded in 1994 and based in Thailand, also made a distinction between forced prostitution and voluntary sex work. GAATW called for decriminalization of prostitution and argued that anti-trafficking efforts must focus on forced prostitution and other forms of abuse and exploitation. GAATW's position was supported by the International Committee for Prostitutes' Rights (ICPR).

The two camps also presented differing views on the notion of consent, in particular "whether non-coerced, adult migrant prostitution should be included in the definition of trafficking" (Gallagher 2001: 984). The Coalition Against Trafficking in Women (CATW) argued that prostitution is never voluntary, because women's consent to sex work is meaningless since they do not realize the exploitation they will experience. The Human Rights Caucus, on the other hand, stated, "No one consents to abduction or forced labor, but an adult woman is able to consent to engage in an illicit activity (such as prostitution). If no one is forcing her to engage in such activity, then trafficking does not exist" (Human Rights Caucus 1999: 5).

With this debate, the definition of trafficking became a battleground between those who consider it possible for sex work to be a voluntary choice and those who consider prostitution to always be forced. In the end, the signatories of the Palermo Protocol rejected the definition championed by the feminist and religious groups represented by the Coalition Against Trafficking in Women (CATW) and defined human trafficking as

> [t]he recruitment, transportation, transfer, harboring or receipt of persons, by means of the threat or use of force or other forms of coercion, of abduction, of fraud, of deception, of abuse of power or of a position of vulnerability or of the giving or receiving of payments or benefits to achieve the consent of a person having control over another person, for the purpose of exploitation. (UN 2000)

In less legalese language, the definition of human trafficking emphasized that force, fraud, or coercion must be present for a particular labor or sexual exploitation to be recognized as human trafficking. This definition was modified in relation to children. In accordance with the 1989 Convention on the Rights of the Child (CRC), the Protocol considered any individual under the age of 18 to be a child. The Protocol stated that the recruitment, transportation, transfer, harboring, or receipt of a child for the purpose of exploitation shall be considered 'trafficking in persons' even if no force or coercion was used. This definition assumes that children, even older teens, have no volition and cannot consent. I have contested this assumption elsewhere (Goździak 2016a).

While the Palermo Protocol provides the first internationally agreed-upon definition of trafficking in human beings, it has elements and foci that have been challenged, including 'exploitation,' the difference between trafficking and smuggling, overemphasis on trafficking of women for sexual exploitation, and the issue most relevant for this discussion: securitization of human trafficking.

The Palermo Protocol focuses on the purpose of human trafficking, namely exploitation. Exploitation is a "difficult concept, certainly never defined in international law, and subject to a variety of interpretations" (Plant 2005: 154). Common sense tells us that exploitation happens when workers are treated unfairly, when they do not receive appropriate remuneration for their labor, and when traffickers take advantage of their vulnerability to extract unfair profits. However, as legal scholars point out, the real challenge is to persuade a jury that the experiences of trafficked persons—high fees that migrant workers often pay recruitment agencies, unexplained deductions from wages, long working hours, insalubrious living and working conditions—meet the muster of criminal offenses. Plant indicates that in Europe, "there are a very small number of egregious cases, where the perpetrators are successfully prosecuted and receive heavy convictions (sometimes accompanied by a civil penalty)" (Plant 2005: 155). The situation is very similar in the United States, where a good proportion of trafficking cases are tried on the basis of immigration violations (smuggling), not under the anti-trafficking law (Shepherd Torg 2006; Kyckelhahn et al 2009; Goździak 2016a).

The Palermo Protocol makes a distinction between trafficking and smuggling with regard to three crucial points: consent, exploitation, and transnationality. Smuggling involves migrants who have consented to being smuggled. Trafficking victims, on the other hand, have either never consented or, if they initially consented, that consent has been rendered meaningless by the coercive, deceptive or abusive actions of the traffickers. Smuggling usually ends with the migrants' arrival at their destination, whereas trafficking involves ongoing exploitation of the victim. It is commonly believed that victims of trafficking tend to be affected more severely and to be in greater need of protection from re-victimization than are smuggled migrants. Personally, I am not sure this distinction has been borne out by empirical data. Moreover, how would we measure the severity of exploitation and suffering of these two groups? And finally, smuggling is always transnational, whereas trafficking can occur within the country of origin of the victim.

Julia O'Connell Davidson (2013) reviewed how some policy-makers, nongovernmental organization (NGO) activists, and academics see trafficking and smuggling. She concluded that, one, trafficking can be a process, whereas smuggling is a one-time transaction, and, two, that trafficking involves 'coercion and deception,' while smuggling is 'voluntary.' These distinctions may appear clear in theory, but in practice it is difficult to distinguish trafficking from smuggling. Most of the trafficking victims I studied started as smuggled individuals, often transported across international borders by family members or friends, but some ended in a severely exploitative situation that was deemed by government authorities to meet the definition of human trafficking.

With the Protocol in place, many international organizations, such as the International Labor Organization (ILO), the United Nations Children's Fund (UNICEF), the International Organization for Migration (IOM), and the European Union (EU), have engaged in vigorous anti-trafficking campaigns. In 2005, the Council of Europe adopted a regional Convention on Action against Trafficking in Human Beings in order to reinforce the provisions of the Palermo Protocol and to ensure its realization in Europe (Osterdahl 2009). In her provocative book *Sex at the Margins*, Laura Augustín named the complex system of anti-trafficking projects and the ever-expanding number of anti-trafficking advocates 'the rescue industry." She argues, along with other authors, that to fight 'modern-day slavery,' faith-based organizations—the main actors in the anti-trafficking field—operate on a rescue-based model. The model involves pursuing "'rescue' operations in which they generally work with law enforcement to 'bust' local brothels suspected of keeping underage girls as prostitutes. The model is to extract or rescue individuals and put them into shelters for 'rehabilitation' and, presumably, their safety" (Augustín 2007).

Focus on Women and Girls

Although the Palermo Protocol includes various forms of labor exploitation, the implementation of the Protocol in various countries has long been plagued by the focus on sex trafficking of women and girls. Trafficking for other forms of labor as well as trafficking of men and boys for sexual or any other form of exploitation received a lot less attention.

Advocates prioritized sex trafficking victims because they match the image of the 'ideal victims'—weak, vulnerable, defenseless women and children.

Originally, the Protocol addressing human trafficking was to be entitled "Trafficking in Women and Children," omitting men entirely. Only later was the phrase "especially women and children" included. The Smuggling Protocol, on the other hand, "has no such coda and no specific emphasis on gender. Smuggled migrants are assumed to be men seeking work elsewhere without proper documentation, while trafficked persons are assumed to be duped victims, usually women" (Kempadoo 2005: 109). This gendered distinction is rooted in stereotypes of women and girls as victims and men and boys as less vulnerable to exploitation. This ideology not only presents a distorted view of women, but also harms men. Trafficked men are invisible. Exploitation of men and boys is not readily recognized and thus is much more difficult to address.

The focus on women and girls is also related to the fact that the trafficking discourse centers on trafficking for sexual exploitation to the detriment of other types of trafficking. Women and girls are considered to be particularly vulnerable to trafficking because in many parts of the world they have low social status, limited access to education, few rights to property, and scarce opportunities to participate in the political process. While low socioeconomic status might indeed be a risk factor for trafficking, highly educated women are not immune to being trafficked. In fact, empirical studies confirm that the trafficking of highly educated women from Eastern Europe and the former Soviet Union is not as rare as the argument linking lack of educational opportunities with trafficking would have us believe (see European Parliament 2000; Kligman and Limoncelli 2005; Morawska 2007). Poverty as a root cause of trafficking also needs to be further explored. Not all poor women and girls resort to migration to improve their economic situation. In the early 2000s, when the anti-trafficking field was holding Eastern European women trafficked for sexual exploitation under a magnifying glass, there were virtually no reports about trafficked Bulgarians despite the fact that Bulgarian women were as poor as Ukrainian or Polish women. In September 2002, at a conference in Brussels, a staff member from the US embassy in Sofia asked me what I thought of the fact that we heard nothing about trafficking of Bulgarians. I did not have an answer, but thought that the Bulgarian case was proof that poverty was not a sole indicator of being at risk for trafficking (Goździak 2015).

The gendered (as well as raced, classed, and sexualized) discourse on human trafficking stems from the current disconnect "between the broad legal definition that embraces any worker who experienced force, fraud, or coercion and the narrow latitude of activist and policy discussion that focuses on sex work" (Mahdavi 2011: 13). It does not result from exceptional vulnerability of women and girls, real or perceived. The centrality of women in the trafficking discourse "maintains the gendered divide around which earlier definitions of trafficking settled and thus reinforces the general, dominant image of trafficking as pertinent only to women's and girls' lives." The concept of gender inequality continues to guide research, "with situations of poor women and girls becoming the main concern of those involved with anti-trafficking work" (Kempadoo 2005: ix).

The disproportionate focus on sex trafficking has resulted in curtailments of migrant women's rights in many parts of the world. As Melissa Ditmore (2008) wrote, Cambodia outlawed prostitution in February 2008 under pressure from the United States. Conflation of sex trafficking with prostitution seriously affected AIDS prevention programs. The US President's Emergency Plan for AIDS Relief (PEPFAR), established under George W. Bush in 2003, required all organizations that received PEPFAR funding to oppose prostitution and trafficking, both of which had been seen as oppressive. The so-called Anti-Prostitution Pledge effectively ended AIDS prevention programs for sex workers (Galusca 2012).

Finally, the gendered dimension of human trafficking relates to broader issues of women and migration. Despite the continued feminization of migration—half of the world's migrants are women (Zlotnik 2013)—there remains a "bias that women and girls need constant male or state protection from harm, and therefore must not be allowed to exercise their right to movement or right to earn a living in a manner they choose" (Kempadoo 2005: 29). "Some countries (e.g., Bangladesh, Myanmar, and Nepal) have even prohibited women from migration because of the fear that they will end up in trouble" (Anker and Liempt 2012: 8). This bias often conflates migration with trafficking and contributes to the notion that women are the main victims of trafficking. Critics have argued that anti-trafficking measures have been used not necessarily to protect women from exploitation, but to police, punish, and racialize female migrants.

TVPA and the Four Ps: Prevention, Protection, Prosecution, and Partnerships

In the United States, trafficking became a focus of activities in the late 1990s when two separate bills were proposed in Congress. Senator Paul Wellstone (D-MN) sponsored a bill that included provisions to prosecute forced labor in all its forms, emphasizing that involuntary servitude was not exclusive to the sex industry but was also liable to occur in agriculture, garment, food, and many other industries. Republican congressman Chris Smith, aided by Laura Lederer, then of the Protection Project, and Gary Haugen of the International Justice Mission, drafted an alternate bill and launched a forceful campaign against Wellstone's proposed legislation. Congressman Smith's bill claimed that Senator Wellstone's "focus on a range of labor issues would distract from combating sex slavery."

In the end, Congress passed the Victims of Trafficking and Violence Protection Act and President Bill Clinton signed it into law on October 28, 2000. This legislation, known as the Trafficking Victims Protection Act (TVPA), was reauthorized in 2003, 2005, 2008, and 2013 (Busch-Armendariz et al. 2018). The TVPA defines human trafficking as:

> the recruitment, harboring, transportation, provision or obtaining of a person for labor or services, through the use of force, fraud, or coercion for the purpose of subjugation to involuntary servitude, peonage, debt bondage, slavery, or commercial sex acts. (TVPA, Section 103[8])

The Act was the product of a tenuous alliance between evangelical Christians and secular feminist anti-trafficking crusaders. Feminist organizations—such as Equity Now and the Protection Project—joined forces in the name of saving the world's women and children. The already-mentioned Laura Lederer, editor of the classic feminist anti-pornography anthology *Take Back the Night*, a former State Department appointee, and current president of Global Centurion, an NGO devoted to fighting modern slavery by focusing on demand, was the major link between feminist and evangelical organizations. She famously defended this alliance, saying that faith-based organizations had introduced "a fresh perspective and biblical mandate to the women's movement. Women's groups don't understand that the partnership on this issue has strengthened them, because they would not be getting attention internationally otherwise" (Crago 2003: 1).

Although the TVPA of 2000 included both sex and labor trafficking in the definition of human trafficking, the US focus on sex trafficking paralleled international anti-trafficking efforts. Combating sexual slavery became a key priority in the Bush administration. The Department of Justice under John Ashcroft spent an average of $100 million annually to fight trafficking domestically and internationally, "a sum that overshadows any other individual nation's contributions to similar efforts" (Soderlund 2005: 67). In recent years, the US government has identified many more cases of trafficking for labor than for sexual exploitation alone. In Fiscal Year 2014, 72 percent of victims were trafficked for labor versus 21 percent for sexual exploitation (ORR 2015), while in 2006, 94 percent of victims were females trafficked for sexual exploitation.

The TVPA initially got lost in the transfer of power from the Clinton to the Bush administration, much to abolitionists' chagrin. Gretchen Soderlund reported that in 2002, the groups behind the TVPA mobilized their constituencies and put pressure on the Bush administration to enforce the provisions of TVPA. Michael Horowitz, former senior fellow at the Hudson Institute and a senior adviser to the Religious Action Center of Reform Judaism, played a key role in the coalition that got the TVPA signed into law. Horowitz wrote to a fellow advocate that it was time to mobilize the administration to get serious about the fight against human trafficking. He worried that, if left to their own devices, sex workers' rights advocates would be teaching "seven-year-old girls how to get their customers to use condoms and to use techniques that make sexual penetration less painful" (Hertzke 2004: 331). In his opinion, the administration had to start supporting anti-trafficking programs aimed at eradicating all forms of prostitution. Horowitz continued to criticize the US government for not enforcing the TVPA in the international arena. "It [the TIP report] is not taken seriously by foreign governments," he said. He also added that the US government response to human trafficking has become "a series of press conferences with no bite" and described the State Department as "a white noise operation" (Neubauer 2012).

The law was aimed at accomplishing what originally came to be known at the "Three Ps": prevention, protection, and prosecution. The fourth P—partnerships—came in much later. Prevention "relates to activities such as public education and job creation intended to keep potential victims out of the clutches of traffickers and away from exploitation," developing "viable economic alternatives to their desperate migration for work" and thus getting to the root causes of human trafficking

(DeStefano 2008). Protection describes a diverse array of assistance programs—housing, financial assistance, medical care, and mental health counseling—available to victims of severe forms of trafficking who meet certain eligibility criteria. Prosecution holds traffickers accountable under criminal law and levies appropriate penalties. Partnership means collaboration between different agencies and actors to prevent trafficking in persons, protect victims, and prosecute perpetrators.

Policy-makers and anti-trafficking advocates regard the TVPA of 2000 and the Trafficking Victims Protection Reauthorization Act of 2003 as the main tools to combat trafficking in persons globally and domestically. The passage of the TVPA launched an entirely new federal bureaucracy to deal with human trafficking. The US Department of State created its Office to Monitor and Combat Trafficking in Persons (J/TIP). Other departments—the Department of Health and Human Services, Department of Justice, US Agency for International Development, Department of Labor, Department of Homeland Security, Department of Education, and Department of Defense—followed and created their own programs to fight human trafficking. In his report titled *Blind Faith*, Senator Coburn called the growing federal anti-trafficking apparatus "wasteful, mismanaged, and duplicative." He has taken issue with the amount of money authorized to combat human trafficking, emphasizing that the dollars spent on anti-trafficking initiatives have grown exponentially—from $31.8 million in 2001 to $185.5 million in 2010—with agencies having difficulty keeping track of their funds (Coburn 2011).

Of all the federal officials leading the anti-trafficking crusade, John Miller, the first director of the US State Department's Office to Monitor and Combat Trafficking in Persons (the TIP Office), was probably the best-known and most written about figure. "Our job under this statute is to end trafficking," Miller stated in 2003. "If America fails to take the lead in rescuing the victims, there's no other nation that will." According to E. Benjamin Skinner, author of *A Crime So Monstrous: Face-to-Face with Modern-day Slavery*, Miller loved the media: "He viewed it as an essential weapon of the new abolitionist movement, and he tended to speak without a filter" (Skinner 2008: 45). Indeed, he did not mince words and had a flair for using sensationalistic phrases to discuss human trafficking. Miller was one of the first people to call human trafficking 'modern-day slavery.' In a conversation in my office, he bemoaned the fact that Colin Powell, the former Secretary of State, would not use the word 'slavery' to describe trafficking in persons. Colin Powell thought the term 'slavery' was too politically charged and emotionally loaded. "The best I was able to do," Miller said, "was to persuade him to use slavery-like conditions."[1] Miller was highly attuned to the political importance of linguistic frames. He argued that the term 'sex worker,' which is preferred by some civil society actors and feminist academics, served "to justify modern-day slavery, [and] dignify the perpetrators and the industries who enslaved [them]" (Bernstein 2007).

Before taking over the TIP Office, Miller, a former member of the House of Representatives from Washington State and a fervent anti-trafficking advocate, chaired the Seattle-based Discovery Institute, a nonpartisan organization focusing, among other things, on the theory of creationism known as intelligent design. He brought the same conservative attitudes to the anti-trafficking enterprise. The Trafficking Victims Protection Reauthorization Act of 2003 elevated Miller's status, raising his rank to ambassador-at-large (DeStefano 2008: 106–107).

John Miller believed that prostitution 'fuels' the increase in sex trafficking. In 2005, a group of human rights activists, lawyers, and researchers challenged Miller's opinion by stating that his views were not supported by valid research and empirical data and that the government's focus on prostitution rather than all forms of labor trafficking was skewing the country's actions. Miller did not listen to the scholars and human rights activists. He squarely focused the administration's policy on the link between prostitution and trafficking: "Sex work causes sex trafficking; thus, eliminating one would eliminate the other," he said. As DeStefano emphasizes, "This policy approach was a dramatic shift from the U.N. Protocol's position, which did not condemn prostitution. Rather it condemned the coercion or deceit used to inveigle and compel a person to do a job, which may or may not be prostitution" (DeStefano 2008: xix).

Miller was also a great supporter of the TIP Reports his office produced. These annual reports rank countries according to a number of indicators listed in Section 108 of the TVPA. Among the criteria are vigorous prosecution of traffickers, extradition of suspects where appropriate, protection of victims, awareness-raising campaigns, cooperation

[1] Personal communication September 2013.

with international efforts aimed at stopping human trafficking, and prosecution of public officials who participate or facilitate trafficking in persons. Many of these reports were met with some controversy. The 2003 report was the first one to involve sanctions, while the 2004 report introduced a watch list—a probationary status of sorts. Many legal scholars and social scientists voiced skepticism about the value of this 'naming and shaming mechanism,' but Miller defended the reports. At a press briefing on June 4, 2004, he said that the country reports were pressing governments to do something about human trafficking: "For example, 24 countries this past year have new, comprehensive anti-trafficking laws. There have been almost 8,000 prosecutions of traffickers worldwide and almost 3,000 convictions" (DeStefano 2008: 125). His successor, Mark P. Lagon, also spoke favorably about the TIP reports despite the fact that the reports continued to be based on anecdotal information and are not grounded in systematic research. In 2008, at a large meeting with stakeholders where he was announcing anticipated financial support for anti-trafficking activities, I asked Ambassador Lagon whether his office planned to support research on trafficking or evaluate the efficacy of the programs the J/TIP Office funded. Not surprisingly, the answer was no. "We might fund an evaluability assessment but do not have any plans to support basic research." Luis CdeBaca, the subsequent director of the TIP Office, stood by the information published in the reports as well. Under his leadership, several evaluation efforts had been undertaken, but the results were not made publicly available.

In 2009, Secretary of State Hilary Rodham Clinton added the fourth P—Partnerships—to the original 3Ps outlined in the TVPA, asserting: "The criminal network that enslaves millions of people crosses borders and spans continents. So, our response must do the same. So, we're committed to building new partnerships with governments and NGOs around the world, because the repercussions of trafficking affect us all" (J/TIP 2009: Introduction). Almost every federal department wanted to be part of the network. New anti-trafficking campaigns were launched, often disregarding previous initiatives and duplicating efforts. The Blue Campaign launched by the Department of Homeland Security in 2010 is an example of one of the latest additions to federal anti-trafficking efforts.

While the J/TIP Office in the State Department has dealt almost exclusively with anti-trafficking overseas—through grants supporting awareness campaigns, training programs, technical assistance aimed at establishing national anti-trafficking laws, and direct services to trafficked persons, mainly women—it nevertheless set a tone for activities at home aimed at trafficking into the United States. Although most people—minors and adults—were trafficked to the United States for labor exploitation, the State Department's focus on sex trafficking has affected the ways trafficked persons are conceptualized. In my book on children and youth trafficked to the United States, I discussed how law enforcement and service providers imagined that the trafficked girls were sexually exploited, whether or not there was actual proof of sexual exploitation (Goździak 2016b).

Expansion of the Concept of Human Trafficking

Protocols and laws providing definitions of human trafficking notwithstanding, different concepts of 'human trafficking' exist in different countries and among stakeholders engaged in anti-trafficking activities (Anker and Liempt 2012). The view of human trafficking continues to expand, allegedly in response to the evolving nature of the modus operandi of traffickers. The label 'trafficking' is often applied to other forms of exploitation, including forced begging, the exploitation of an individual in criminal activities, illegal adoption, and forced marriage (Thomson 2016). New populations are included: child soldiers, 'bush wives,' underage brides, etc.

Trafficking is often overemphasized within the general debates on migration. Some destination countries or actors within the international migration regime such as Frontex, the EU border management agency, use trafficking and smuggling as excuses to develop more restrictive immigrant and refugee admission policies. The recent 'refugee crisis' in Europe is but one example of the expanding human trafficking narrative that criminalizes or victimizes migrants and refugees. In fact, in some countries, national anti-trafficking strategies are directly linked to the overall migration management policies (e.g., Bangladesh, Nepal, Laos). These policies adversely affect women and youth. The main strategy of the Nepali government to prevent trafficking of women was to ban migration of females under the age of 30 to the Gulf states for domestic work (Goździak 2016c). The Government of Laos embraced various anti-trafficking initiatives to control labor migration, especially outmigration of young people (Huijsmans 2011).

Some conceptualize human trafficking as 'modern-day slavery' (Miers 2003; Ould 2004; Bales 2005; Smith 2007). Kevin Bales is possibly the most fervent advocate of presenting human trafficking as modern form of slavery. He argues that new slavery involves "the complete control of a person for economic exploitation by violence or threat of violence" (Bales 2000: 462). Proponents of the usage of the term 'slavery' claim that it "guarantees a wider audience" in the anti-trafficking fight (van der Anker 2004). Indeed, the United Nations, national governments of different countries, as well as advocacy organizations have used testimonies and images of women and girls subjected to extreme violence in the ever-expanding awareness-raising campaigns and training programs. Others, however, caution against sensationalizing human trafficking and are critical of the moralizing agenda reminiscent of the nineteenth century 'white slave panic' (Doezema 2000; Anderson 2004; O'Connell Davidson 2006).

Personally, I do not favor sensational stories, especially when they are supplanted where data stemming from rigorous research should be cited. Moreover, stretching the label 'human trafficking' to the utmost and using it to cover a wide range of social wrongs and human rights abuses does not serve the victims well. Many negative consequences stem from the ways trafficking is conceptualized and operationalized. Trafficked persons are often depicted as victims without agency and referred to patronizing support programs (Nanu 2010). Some survivors are re-trafficked when they try "to escape mindless jobs in International Organization for Migration (IOM) return programs" (Anker and Liempt 2012: 4). There is lack of protection in cases where trafficked persons cooperate with law enforcement against their captors (Hopkins 2005, cited in Anker and Liempt 2012). In my view, instead of stretching the concept of human trafficking, we should aim at distinguishing different forms of exploitation and abuse in order to appropriately tailor policy and program responses.

In the subsequent chapters, the readers will also realize that no matter how narrowly or broadly trafficking in person is defined, it is very often linked to different security issues.

References

Anderson, Bridget. 2004. Migrant Domestic Workers and Slavery. In *The Political Economy of New Slavery*, ed. Christien van den Anker, 107–117. Basingstoke: Palgrave Macmillan.

Anker, Christien van den and Ilse van Liempt. 2012. *Human Rights and Migration. Trafficking for Forced Labor*. Basingstoke: Palgrave Macmillan.
Augustin, Laura María. 2007. *Sex at the Margins: Migration, Labor Markets and the Rescue Industry*. London: Zed Books.
Bales, Kevin. 2000. Expandable People: Slavery in the Age of Globalization. *Journal of International Affairs* 53 (2): 461–484.
Bales, Kevin. 2005. *Understanding Global Slavery*. Berkeley, CA: University of California Press.
Berman, Jacqueline. 2003. (Un)popular Strangers and Crises (un)bounded: Discourses of Sex Trafficking, the European Political Community and the Panicked State of the Modern State. *European Journal of International Relations* 9 (1): 37–86.
Bernstein, Elizabeth. 2007. The Sexual Politics of the 'New Abolitionism'. *Differences: Journal of Feminist Cultural Studies* 18 (3): 128–151.
Busch-Armendariz, Noel Bridget, Maura Nsonwu, and Laurie Cook Hefferon. 2018. *Human Trafficking: Applying Research, Theory, and Case Studies*. Los Angeles: Sage.
Butler, Josephine. Letters Collection. 1989. The Women's Library Collection at LSE.
Bullough, Vern, and Bonnie Bullough. 1987. *Women and Prostitution: A Social History*. New York: Prometheus Books.
Clinton, William J. Memorandum for the Secretary of State, the Attorney General, the Administrator of the Agency for International Development, the Director of the United States Information Agency, March 11, 1998, Subject: Steps to Combat Violence Against Women and Trafficking in Women and Girls, reprinted in 3 TRANSN'L ORGANIZED CRIME 214 (1997).
Coburn, Tom. 2011. Blind Faith: How Congress Is Failing Trafficking Victims. Office of Tom Coburn, U.S. Senate.
Crago, Anna-Louise. 2003. Unholy Alliance. Available at https://www.alternet.org/story/15947/unholy_alliance.
Derks, Anushka. 2000. From White Slaves to Trafficking Survivors: Notes on the Trafficking Debate. Working Paper 00–02. Princeton: Center for Migration and Development, Princeton University.
DeStefano, Anthony M. 2008. *The War on Human Trafficking: U.S. Policy Assessed*. New Brunswick, NJ: Rutgers University Press, xix.
Ditmore, Melissa. 2008. Sex Work, Trafficking: Understanding the Difference. *Rewire News Group* May 6, 2008. Available: https://rewirenewsgroup.com/article/2008/05/06/sex-work-trafficking-understanding-difference/.
Doezema, Jo. 1999. Loose women or lost women? The re-emergence of the myth of white slavery in contemporary discourses of trafficking in women. *Gender Issues* 18: 23–50.

Dozema, Jo. 2000. Loose Women or Lost Women? The Re-emergence of the Myth of White Slavery in Contemporary Discourses of Trafficking in Women. *Gender Issues* 18 (1): 23–50.

Doezema, Jo. 2002. Who Gets to Choose? Coercion, Consent, and the UN Trafficking Protocol. *Gender and Development* 10 (1): 20–27.

Doezema, Jo. 2005. Now You See Her, Now You Don't: Sex Workers at the UN Trafficking Protocol Negotiations. *Social & Legal Studies* 14: 61–89.

European Parliament. 2000. Trafficking in Women. Working Paper. Available at http://www.europarl.europa.eu/workingpapers/libe/pdf/109_en.pdf.

Gallagher, Anne. 2001. Human Rights and the New UN Protocols on Trafficking and Migrant Smuggling: A Preliminary Analysis. *Human Rights Quarterly* 23: 975–1004.

Galusca, Roxana. 2012. Slave Hunters, Brothel Busters, and Feminist Interventions: Investigative Journalists as Anti-Sex-Trafficking Humanitarians. *Feminist Formations* 24 (2): 1–24. https://doi.org/10.1353/ff.2012.0018.

Goldscheider, Eric. 2000. Prostitutes Work, But Do They Consent? http://departments.bloomu.edu/crimjust/pages/articles/sex_tourism.htm.

Goździak, Elżbieta M. 2015. *In Search of Data and Research on Human Trafficking: Analysis of Research-Based Literature (2008–2014)*, July. Washington, DC.

Goździak, Elżbieta M. 2016a. Of Will or Force? Contesting Assumptions about Child Trafficking. In *Contested Childhoods: Growing Up in Migrancy*, eds. Marie Louise Seeberg and Elżbieta M. Goździak. New York: Springer.

Goździak, Elżbieta M. 2016b. *Trafficked Children and Youth in the United States. Reimagining Survivors*. New Brunswick, NJ: Rutgers University Press.

Goździak, Elżbieta M. 2016c. *Trafficking Survivors Return Home: Case study of Nepal*. Washington, DC: ISIM/Georgetown University.

Goździak, Elżbieta M., and Micah N. Bump. 2008. *Data and Research on Human Trafficking: Bibliography of Research-Based Literature*. Report to NIJ, October.

Hertzke, Allan D. 2004. *Freeing God's Children: The Unlikely Alliance for Human Rights*. Lanham, MD: Rowman and Littlefield, 331. Cited in Soderlund, "Running from the Rescuers".

Huijsmans, Roy. 2011. The Theatre of Human Trafficking: A Global Discourse on Lao Stages. *The International Journal of Social Quality* 1 (2): 66–84.

Human Rights Caucus. 1999. Recommendations and Commentary on the Draft Protocol to Prevent, Suppress and Punish Trafficking in Persons, Especially Women and Children, Supplementing the United Nations Convention against International Organized Crime.

Julia, O'Connel Davidson. 2006. Will the Real Sex Slave Please Stand Up? *Feminist Review* 83: 4–22.

Kelly, Elizabeth, and Linda Regan. 2000. Stopping Trafficking, Exploring the Extent of, and Responses to, Trafficking in Women for Sexual Exploitation in the UK. Police Research Series 125 London: Home Office.

Kempadoo, Kamala (ed.). 2005. *Trafficking and Prostitution Reconsidered: New Perspectives on Migration, Sex Work and Human Rights*. Boulder, CO: Paradigm Publishers.

Kligman, Gail, and Stephanie Limoncelli. 2005. Trafficking Women after Socialism: To, Through and From Eastern Europe. *Social Politics: International Studies in Gender, State and Society* 12 (1): 118–140.

Kyckelhahn, Tracey, Allen J. Beck, and Thomas H. Cohen. 2009. *Characteristics of Suspected Human Trafficking Incidents, 2007–08*. Washington, DC: Bureau of Justice Statistics. http://www.bjs.gov/content/pub/pdf/cshti08.pdf.

Lee, Maggy. 2011. *Trafficking and Global Crime Control*. London: Sage.

Mahdavi, Pardis. 2011. *Gridlock: Labor, Migration, and Human Trafficking in Dubai*. Stanford: Stanford University Press.

Miers, Suzanne. 2003. *Slavery in the Twentieth Century: The Evolution of a Global Problem*. Walnut Creek, CA: Alta Mira Press.

Meshkovska, Biljana, and Melissa Siegel. 2015. Female Sex Trafficking: Conceptual Issues, Current Debates, and Future Directions. *Journal of Sex Research* 52 (4): 380–395.

Morawska, Ewa. 2007. Trafficking into and from Eastern Europe. In *Human Trafficking*, ed. Maggy Lee. London and New York: Routledge.

Nanu, Cezara. 2010. Preventing Trafficking in Human Beings: The Case of Moldova. In *Human Trafficking in Europe*, eds. Gillian Wylie and Penelope McRedmond, 142–163. Palgrave Macmillan.

Neubauer, Chuck. 2012. Top Human Traffickers Need Not Fear Obama. *Washington Times*, July 29.

O'Connell, Davidson. 2013. Troubling Freedom: Migration, Debt, and Modern Slavery. *Migration Studies* 1 (2): 176–195.

Office of Refugee Resettlement. 2015. Annual Report to Congress FY 2014, Washington.

Ollus, Natalia. 2015. Regulating Forced Labor and Combating Human Trafficking: the Relevance of Historical Definitions in a Contemporary Perspective. *Crime Law Soc Change* 63: 221–246.

Osterdahl, Inger. 2009. International Countermeasures Against Trafficking. In *Human Trafficking and Human Security*, ed. Anna Jonsson, 67–92. London: Routledge.

Ould, David. 2004. Trafficking and International Law. In *The Political Economy of New Slavery*, ed. Christien van den Anker, 55–74. Basingstoke: Palgrave Macmillan.

Outshoorn, Joyce. 2015. The Trafficking Policy Debates. In *Global Human Trafficking. Critical Issues and Contexts*, ed. Molly Dragiewicz, 7–22. London: Routledge.

"Partnerships." Office to Monitor and Combat Trafficking Persons (J/TIP), U.S. Department of State. Available at http://www.state.gov/j/tip4p/partner/index.htm. Accessed August 15, 2014.

Plant, Roger. 2005. Forced Labor, Slavery and Human Trafficking: When Do Definitions Matter? *Anti-Trafficking Review* 5: 153–157.

Shepherd Torg, Cynthia. 2006. Human Trafficking Enforcement in the United States. 14 TUL. J. INT'L & COMP. L. 503.

Skinner, Benjamin E. 2008. *A Crime So Monstrous: Face-to-Face with Modern-Day Slavery*. New York: Free Press.

Smith, Danny. 2007. *Slavery Now—And Then*. Eastbourne: Kingsway Publications.

Soderlund, Gretchen. 2005. Running from the Rescuers: New U.S. Crusades against Sex Trafficking and the Rhetoric of Abolition. *NWSA Journal* 17 (3): 64–87.

Steele, Abby. 2006. Insecurity and Opportunity in Colombia: Linking Civil War and Human Trafficking. In *Trafficking and the Global Sex Industry*, eds. Karen Beeks and Delila Amir, 77–96. Lanham, MD: Lexington Books.

Thomson, Kristy. 2016. International and European Standards in Relation to Victims and Survivors of Human Trafficking. In *Human Trafficking: The Complexities of Exploitation*, ed. Margaret Molloch and Paul Rogby. Edinburgh: Edinburgh University Press.

United Nations. 2000. UN Protocol to Prevent, Suppress, and Punish Trafficking in Persons, Especially Women and Children.

Valenti, Jessica. 2010. *The Purity Myth: How America's Obsession with Virginity Is Hurting Young Women*. Berkeley, CA: Seal Press.

van den Anker, Christien (ed.). 2004. *The Political Economy of New Slavery*. Basingstoke: Palgrave Macmillan.

Vlassis, Dimitri. 2001. The United Nations Convention Against Transnational Organized Crime and Its Three Protocols: Development and Outlook. Unpublished paper cited in Ann Gallagher.

Wijers, Marjan, and Lin Lap-Chew. 1997. *Trafficking in Women: Forced Labor and Slavery-Like Practices in Marriage, Domestic Labor and Prostitution*. Amersfoort, The Netherlands: La Strada International.

Woodiwiss, Michael, and Dick Hobbs. 2008. Organized Evil and the Atlantic Alliance: Moral Panics and the Rhetoric of Organized Crime Policing in America and Britain. *British Journal of Criminology* 49 (1): 106–128.

Zlotnik, Hania. 2013. Population: Crowd Control. *Nature* 501: 30–31.

CHAPTER 3

Human Trafficking as a Security Threat

Since September 11, 2001, the concept of security has been invoked constantly. Emphasis on endless security threats has usurped the international discourses, displacing all other phenomena to the margins of public scrutiny (Goldstein 2010). Indeed, we hear and read about a multitude of security threats, including terrorism (Mueller 2006), national security threats (Richards 2012; Goldman 2001), international migration (Adamson 2006), and environmental threats (Barnett 2003).

But what do we mean by security? Does a challenge to national identity, for example, posed by the increased presence of minority or immigrant populations, constitute a threat to national security? What about labor migrants forced into indentured servitude or young women coerced into the sex industry? Do they pose a security threat? To whom?

It is often assumed that 'security' is a simple concept, the meaning of which we all know (Waever 1996). Nothing could be further from the truth. The term security is often used to describe the degree of resistance to, or protection from, harm. In scientific and political debates, there is frequently a tension between collective security and individual security and between external and internal security. Security debates entail negative and positive dialogues. Negative dialogues focus on danger, risk, and threat, while positive dialogues center on opportunities, interests, and profits. Negative dialogues need military equipment, armies, and law enforcement, including border controland immigration detention. Positive dialogues need social capital, education, and social interaction.

E. M. Goździak, *Human Trafficking as a New (In)Security Threat*,
https://doi.org/10.1007/978-3-030-62873-4_3

It is not my intention to provide an in-depth discussion of existing definitions of and debates about security. As an anthropologist and a migration scholar, I do not have the requisite expertise in security studies to do such an exercise justice. Instead, I will concentrate on the securitization of human trafficking, and more broadly international migration. But let's begin by looking at the etymology of the word 'security' and its meaning(s).

The Origins and Meaning of 'Security'

The origins of the word 'security' date back to the mid-fifteenth century. Deriving from Latin *securitas* and *securus*, the term 'security' denotes a 'condition of being secure,' and 'free from care,' respectively.

According to the Collins English Dictionary and Thesaurus (1992), "Security may be considered as assured freedom from poverty or want, precautions taken to ensure against theft, espionage or a person or thing that secures or guarantees." In this conceptualization, "security implies a stable, relatively predictable environment in which an individual or group may pursue its ends without disruption or harm and without fear of such disturbance or injury" (Fischer et al. 2004: 21).

Scholars of international relations typically locate security and the ability to create it within the state. Ole Waever posits that the 'traditionalists' argue that the concept of security—as used in security studies or in debates on security policies—has no basic meaning independent of the state. Citing R.B.J. Walker (1990), Waever points out that our political concepts have been shaped by the modern, nation-state context and that it would be naïve to assume that the concept of 'security' can be detached from the concept of 'state.' He writes:

> The two concepts are already present in each other. If this were to be denied, both state and security would have to be reified and naturalized for them to be seen as necessary, ahistorical, constant entities. (Waever 1996: 105)

The 'traditionalist' view presents security as pertaining solely to matters of military affairs, with defense of the state being the single most important factor in defining a particular crisis as security threat (Buzan et al. 1998; Chipman 1992). In this conceptualization of security, the state possesses the exclusive right to both define and impose 'security.' The state is therefore authorized to assess risk and control dissent. These actions are perceived as its 'moral duty' and provision of security is equated with provision of social welfare (see Bratich 2006; Hay and Andrejevic 2006). This viewpoint corresponds with the Cold War era conceptualization of security when the notion was closely linked to the autonomy of the territorial nation-state where physical frontiers demarcated friend from foe and war from peace. As Burgess and colleagues write (2007), in this sense, security was tightly attached to the political and geographical borders and understood as protection of the state against foreigners who sought to harm national interests.

The non-traditionalists reject the traditionalists' insistence on using military treats as the sole criterion to use the label 'security' (e.g., Wrever et al. 1993). While they oppose the traditionalists' views of security, the non-traditionalists have not reached a consensus on what security means either. Sarah Tarry (2009) distinguishes two camps within the non-traditionalists, namely 'wideners' and 'deepeners.' The wideners argue that a predominantly military definition does not acknowledge that economic, environmental, and social threats endanger the lives of individuals and as a consequence the survival of states. The deepeners, on the other hand, ask the question of whose security is being threatened and support the construction of a definition that allows for individual or structural referent objects, as opposed to the state. Tarry posits that a definition that is excessively broad may limit the analytical usefulness of the concept.

Some scholars contend that the concept of security needs to be expanded because of a declining significance of geographical boundaries. Michael Klare and Daniel Thomas (1994), for example, perceive state actors to be less capable of responding to global problems such as environmental degradation or financial crises. As a result, they advocate a concept of 'world security' that accounts for the global nature of contemporary problems. They firmly believe that nonmilitary threats—ecological, economic, demographic—pose serious challenges to the contemporary world. Furthermore, they argue that nonmilitary risks pose equal or greater threats to people's security even in countries and regions where armed conflict remains constant.

Although today the concept of security encompasses the protection of communities and individuals from internal violence, not just attacks by foreign enemies, the concept of national security—introduced by the US President Harry S. Truman at the end of World War II in 1949—is used more frequently in the context of human trafficking and irregular migration than any other conceptualizations of the term. Khalid Koser (2011), a migration scholar, argues that "the perception of migration as a threat to national security has certainly heightened in recent years, in part in response to the rapid rise in the number of international migrants (…) and especially of 'irregular' or 'illegal' migrants." Ironically, migration from Europe has been considered to be an opportunity, while immigration to Europe or the United States is often perceived as a security threat.

Human trafficking and terrorism

It is often implied that the terrorist attacks on the United States on September 11, 2001 were the reason for connecting human trafficking, a crime not normally associated with national security, with the need to protect the nation (see Stinson 2012). However, the framing of human trafficking as a security threat is part of a much broader attempt to portray international migration as a security risk. Indeed, once it was announced that the nineteen hijackers were foreign nationals, those critical of the US immigration system argued that the government must use all available means to protect the national security of the country. The critics called for "enhancing and enlarging the border security functions of the Immigration and Naturalization Service (INS)" (Chebel d'Appolonia 2012: 1). Within a few days, the Immigration and Nationality Act (INA) was adopted and a series of reforms aimed at implementing immigration restrictions, including detention of foreign-born individuals without charge, began.

Europe followed suit. On September 20, 2001, the Council of the European Union called for strengthening of surveillance measures, including vigilance in issuing residency permits and systematic checking of identity papers, under Article 2.3 of the Schengen Convention. The bombings of Madrid on March 11, 2004, and London on July 7, 2005, further consolidated the national security policies in Europe.

Unfortunately, securitization of migrants and migration is nothing new. Germans residing in the United Kingdom during World War II were interned on the grounds that they may have been 'fifth columnists' (Koser 2011). In the United States, some 120,000 Japanese Americans were forcibly relocated and placed in concentration camps during World War II; approximately 62% were US citizens. Canada followed suit, relocating

21,000 of its Japanese residents (history.com 2009). Kurdish and Algerian diasporas were linked to terrorist attacks in Western Europe during the 1970s and 1980s (Koser 2011).

Recently, however, the links between irregular migration or human smuggling, often conflated with human trafficking, and national or regional security are presented more and more frequently. In the United States, the sitting president considers El Salvador, Haiti, and a myriad of African states 'shithole countries' (Woodhouse 2018). He has banned travel from several Muslim-majority countries and the US Supreme Court, in a ruling 5–4, upheld the ban (Siddiqui 2018). Trump also said that immigrants in the country illegally are responsible for tens of thousands of crimes (Horsley 2018), although his former Chief of Staff, John Kelly, in an interview with the National Public Radio (NPR), acknowledged that most people crossing the border illegally do not pose a security threat (Burnett and Gonzales 2018).

John Kelly's assertion is not shared by others who previously spoke about the relationship between human trafficking and security. John P. Torres, who served as deputy assistant director for smuggling and public safety in the US Bureau of Immigration and Customs Enforcement (ICE) in the Bush administration, told the House Judiciary Subcommittee on Immigration that human smuggling and trafficking into the United States constituted a significant risk to national security and public safety. He also indicated that well-established smuggling and trafficking networks facilitate entry of illegal aliens and criminals into the United States. In my own research, I have primarily seen family members, friends, and neighbors assisting undocumented youth in crossing the US-Mexico border. Some of these young people were later trafficked or deemed to be trafficked, again not by organized criminal networks but rather by unscrupulous employers, often their own family members (Goździak 2016b).

Several researchers, especially graduate students, *believe* [my emphasis] in the connection between human trafficking and terrorism. Interestingly, they all invoke Christine Dolan, a journalist, who writes and speaks about human trafficking. Sandra Keefer (2006), a Colonel in the US Army, in her master's thesis refers to a presentation made by Christine Dolan at a "Terrorism Nexus" seminar hosted by the World Affairs Council of Washington, DC, to emphasize a direct link between human trafficking and terrorism. Elsie Gonzalez (2013) also quotes Christine Dolan and a handful of other journalists as well as (*sic!*) episodes of the HBO show

The Wire to argue that terrorist groups such as Al-Qaeda use human trafficking to replace traditional sources of funding. She posits that proceeds from human trafficking are replacing contributions from rich donors that ended due to US government's efforts to stop money laundering. Sarah Anderson (2013), at the time a doctoral student at Nova Southeastern University in Florida, mentioned Christine Dolan and her report *Shattered Innocence, Millennium Holocaust* in a 2013 blog post. Based, apparently, on a nine-week study tour throughout Europe, in which Dolan interviewed over 500 local people, including children, pimps, police, and prostitutes, the report does not seem to be available online or in libraries, but Dolan talked about it at numerous campuses and seems to have captured the imaginations of students.

I have heard Christine Dolan made the same claim when she spoke at Georgetown University in 2005. In addition to financing terrorist activities, Dolan argued, terrorists use transportation networks of human smugglers and human traffickers to move operatives. According to Dolan, human trafficking is enabling international criminals to play into a wider field of international drug trafficking, weapons and arms dealing, and even piracy. Khalid Koser (2011) counters this argument and suggests that there is very little evidence from any country in the world that there is a greater concentration of terrorists or potential terrorists among migrant or trafficked populations than among local populations. But even if we assume that there might be some logic to the assertions that human trafficking and terrorism are closely connected, I would like to see empirical evidence. However, empirical research in the human trafficking field is still scarce. The anti-trafficking discourse is often dominated by ideology. In academic writing about human trafficking, canons of scientific inquiry are frequently suspended and research deliberately skewed to serve a particular political agenda (Weitzer 2005, 2007).

There are of course exceptions. One such exception is research conducted by Pardis Mahdavi. In her book *From Trafficking to Terror* (Mahdavi 2014), Mahdavi uses empirical research in the United Arab Emirates (UAE), Washington, DC, and California to show how the socially constructed 'war on terror' and 'war on trafficking' are inextricably linked in discourses that often conflate the two phenomena and help perpetuate anti-Muslim sentiments. Furthermore, Mahdavi shows how the rhetoric that stems from the trafficking and terror paradigm has led to:

> policies, discourses, and responses that (1) paint all Muslims and Middle Easterners as "terrifying Muslims" (Rana 2011); (2) portray women, particularly women in the Middle East, or those interacting with "terrifying Muslim men" as without agency and in desperate need of saving; and (3) can be used as anti-immigration means and sentiments (Mahdavi 2014: 74).

Much of the discussions of linkages between human trafficking and terrorism come from conservative outfits such as the Jamestown Foundation. The Foundation indicates that smuggling and trafficking routes provide a number of avenues for potential terrorists to enter the United States. Writing for the Foundation's online publication—*Terrorism Monitor*—Thomas Davidson (2005) stated:

> One of the most common routes is through Havana, Cuba where terrorists could be provided with false documents such as Central American or even European passports. (…) A number of Arabs, Middle Easterners, and other Muslims are still using Central America and parts of South America as jumping off points. (…) the Salafi network in Mexico currently runs from the southernmost state of Chiapas to the northern Mexican border. (…)

Davidson does not indicate the scale of this alleged trafficking of terrorists. Analysis of publicly available databases such as the former Human Trafficking Law Project database at the University of Michigan or the current Human Trafficking Data.org do not include any cases tried under laws related to terrorism or national security.

Human Trafficking and Organized Crime

During a training for Transportation Security Administration (TSA) agents, baggage handlers, and restaurant workers at a large international airport in the United States, I heard trainers describe traffickers as 'restless merchants of modern slavery' who operate 'alien stash houses,' and deal and barter slaves with little retribution across vast international networks. Journalists portray traffickers as "thick-necked, beady-eyed thugs, members of organized crime gangs like the Albanian or Russian mob, the Italian mafia, the Japanese yakuza, Chinese triads or the Hell's Angels" (Malarek 2004). Activists elevate traffickers to an evil, powerful, calculating, and all-knowing entity (Molland 2011). International organizations and academic writers indicate that the traffickers' highly organized criminal networks span the world and are able to adjust to ever-changing environments and demands (UNODC 2000; Shelly 2010).

Many authors (e.g., Aronowitz et al. 2010; Shelly 2010) focus on the alleged connections between sophisticated, organized crime networks and human trafficking despite the fact that there is scant empirical data to support this view. Researchers make this connection based on a variety of disparate facts: People of different nationalities are often part of the same group of trafficked victims, trips over a long distance require a well-oiled organization, substantial amounts of money are involved, itineraries are able to change quickly, legal services are available on a moment's notice, and traffickers are able to speedily react to counter-offensives mounted by law enforcement agencies (Bruckert and Parent 2002). Europol, the European Union's law enforcement agency, has developed these arguments (Salt 2000), but many others share these opinions (see Taibly 2001; Juhasz 2000; Aronowitz et al. 2010; Shelly 2010). The US Department of State reiterates these assertions, describing how traffickers enjoy virtually no risk of prosecution by using surreptitious modes of transportation and communication. Such criminals frequently avoid punishment by operating in places where there is little rule of law, a lack of anti-trafficking legislation, poor enforcement of such laws, and widespread corruption. Some researchers believe there is a close connection between organized crime and trafficking for sexual exploitation due to the close involvement of criminal organizations at various levels of the expansive sex industry (See Shannon 1999; Caldwell et al. 1999).

On the other end of the spectrum are scholars who "have questioned the assumptions behind the organization and transnationality in the trafficking-as-organized crime thesis," writes Maggie Lee, citing Hobbs and Dunningham, Huysmans, Finckenauer, Loader, Levi, and Woodiwiss and Hobbs. Lee explains further that the preoccupation with "external, alien actors, cultures, and organizations"—such as the Russian Mafia, Colombian cartels, Jamaican Yardies, and Chinese triads—is "part of the long-standing intellectual tradition of a criminology of the other, of the threatening outcast, the fearsome stranger, the excluded and the embittered" (Lee 2011: 90).

In my own research on trafficking of adolescents and young adults into the United States (Goździak 2016b), I have seen no evidence of large, organized criminal networks' involvement in the 'trafficking' of the young people I studied. Unlike Amanda in the movie *Taken*, none of the young people in my study were kidnapped or whisked away by criminals whom they had never met before. Most were smuggled across the Mexico-US border by close family members, parents, older siblings, or neighbors. Those that came from Africa entered the United States on a tourist visa, in some cases accompanied by their parents, and were left in the United States with extended family members. Law enforcement, however, saw all those involved in the youngsters' trafficking as part of an international mafia. These officials criminalized the adolescents and young adults' families, regarding them as part of the trafficking chain regardless of what role, if any, they played in the trafficking ordeal. These perceptions about organized crime syndicates are pervasive in illegal migration debates despite the fact that empirical evidence points in a different direction. "While organized crime is certainly involved in many illegal human transfers," writes Raimo Väyrynen (2003: 35), "they can also take place without the criminal contribution. Moreover, many smuggling rings are more like small enterprises run by a group of relatives or acquaintances."

More recently, I have seen young people fleeing widespread violence in the northern triangle of Central America (Honduras, Guatemala, and El Salvador) (Goździak 2015). As I document in Chapter 4, gangs and cartels facilitated the young people's migration to the United States, but more often than not the youths were fleeing violence perpetrated by criminal networks within their countries of origin and were seeking safe haven and peaceful lives in the United States.

I think the connections made between human trafficking and terrorisms and human trafficking and organized crime stem from the fact that human trafficking is imagined by many mainly as large-scale organized crime networks and multibillion-dollar business. While criminal elements are obviously present in human trafficking and traffickers do profit from exploiting victims, human trafficking also involves non-criminal networks, at least not large, organized criminal cartels, but familial and social networks that are perceived by 'trafficked' people as helpers facilitating clandestine migration (Goździak 2016b). These are very different social phenomena and their existence needs to be both acknowledged and understood.

Securitization of Human Trafficking and Migration

Although advocates working with victims of trafficking in persons often think about human trafficking as a human rights issue, let's not forget that the Palermo Protocols on human trafficking and smuggling are part of the UN Convention against Transnational Organized Crime. They were not designed as human rights instruments, but rather as mechanisms to facilitate interstate cooperation in combating organized crime (Shoaps 2013). In fact, over the years, the trafficking protocol has received much criticism for being overly focused on criminal investigation and prosecution at the cost of meaningfully protecting trafficked victims (Hathaway 2008). In a foreword to the Convention, Kofi Annan, the former UN Secretary-General, linked the perpetrators of human trafficking to terrorists, criminals, and drug dealers who undo the good works of civil society and threaten our security.

After the passage of the Palermo Protocols on human trafficking and smuggling, the linkage between human trafficking and national security became quite prominent (Anker and van Liempt 2012); trafficking was re-framed from a human rights issue to a national security threat. In the United States, the declaration on the 'War on Trafficking' by the Bush administration was the first step in the securitization process (Stinson 2012). Scholars criticized the way the US government addressed the linkage between human trafficking and national security (Desyllas 2007; Soderlund 2005; Haynes 2007), but the general public was convinced that sex trafficking was connected to terrorism and illegal immigration, both of which posed a threat to national security. It is ironic that trafficking for labor exploitation has not been tied to national security the same way trafficking for sexual exploitation has, at least not in the United States and in Europe. Is it because the United States depends on a cheap, often undocumented and vulnerable to exploitation, labor force?

Although the Palermo Protocols make clear distinction between human trafficking and smuggling, many policy-makers use the term 'people trafficker' and 'smuggler' interchangeably. This conflation of terms has been quite visible when policy-makers talk about those who aid refugees across the Mediterranean (McQuade 2015). Indeed, smuggling networks play a key role in the migration that has been unfolding in the Mediterranean in the past few years. Luigi Achilli of the Migration Policy Centre, who had conducted interviews with migrants on the different Mediterranean routes—Western Mediterranean via Morocco and Spain, Eastern Mediterranean via Turkey and Greece, and Central Mediterranean via Italy and Malta—described these networks as small and highly heterogeneous organizations, largely family-based, that don't have solid hierarchies and have entered into partnerships with one another for short periods of time. They do not necessarily exploit their clients and, sometimes, the smuggler and the customer are the same person as asylum seekers may work as recruiters, 'passeurs' or intermediaries (Achilli 2017). Smuggling networks are thus deeply enmeshed within migratory flows. A truly effective answer to human smuggling would require the EU and its member states to concentrate on reducing 'demand' more than curbing 'supply,' Mr. Achilli concluded.

Jasper Gilardi (2020) also underscores the complex nature of the relationship between smugglers and clandestine migrants:

> Despite the illicit nature of their work and being cast as villains in the public eye, smugglers have complex, multifaceted relationships with their migrant clients. At times, the relationship can be mutually beneficial or even lifesaving; at others, it can be predatory and dangerous.

Gilardi points out an important distinction that should be drawn between smugglers and human traffickers: "smugglers have clients while traffickers have captives" (Gilardi 2020). Prospective migrants turn to smugglers when legal migration pathways are limited, borders are closed, and clandestine routes difficult to navigate without a guide. Smuggling and trafficking often overlap and the relationship may evolve from smuggler to trafficker along the way. However, migrants' relationship with smugglers is not devoid of vulnerabilities, but doesn't always turn into trafficking. We actually do not have much empirical data on how often smuggling becomes trafficking.

In my own research in Hungary, I have seen and heard about many ordinary Hungarians who were driving refugees to Austria since Hungary had no interest in considering asylum claims from Middle Eastern refugees when they arrived at the railway stations in Budapest and Debrecen in the summer of 2015. While many refugees and Hungarian volunteers assisting asylum seekers were often surprised at the high prices the drivers were charging, most considered them to be entrepreneurs, not traffickers. This is not to say that smuggling operations always end well. In

August 2015, the Hungarian police arrested four smugglers, three Bulgarians, and one Afghan, when a lorry with 71 dead bodies was dumped in Austria (Harding and Nolan 2015). In 2019, all four men received a 30-year sentence (Dunai 2019).

The 'refugee crisis' in Europe has affected the discourse on trafficking. When forced migrants sought safe haven in Europe in 2015, the discourse focused on smuggling. Eurostat said that nearly 90,000 unaccompanied children sought asylum in Europe in 2015, fleeing war and poverty in the Middle East and Africa to reach a place of safety (Gale 2016). They estimated that of those, 10,000 minors were at risk for being trafficked (Nickerson 2016). In an advocacy brief, UNICEF wrote that many of the unaccompanied and separated children left the centers where they were cared for within a short period of time and there was no information on what happened to them afterward. UNICEF added, however, that:

> This does not mean that they are (all) necessarily trafficked. As children do not trust that their best interests will prevail in the current procedures, they may take matters into their own hands. Some of them arrive in Europe under pressure to earn money to pay back smugglers and or assist family back home. They might try to unite with extended family, peers or move for other reasons to chosen destination countries. The risk of exploitation exists but little evidence is available on whether children who leave centers navigate successfully through such risks or indeed end up exploited and in a worse off situation. (UNICEF, nd: 4)

I would also like to emphasize that many of these 'children' are really adolescents with a lot of agency and their 'disappearance' might mean that they are searching for better solutions to their plight on their own, without the help of care centers and assistance programs staff. I will return to this issue in Chapter 7 when I discuss unaccompanied children and adolescents seeking refuge in Europe.

One thing seems certain: Those who help migrants to cross international borders are increasingly considered traffickers, not smugglers. Even casual observations of policy debates in the United States and various European countries suggest that smuggling has been re-framed as human trafficking. In my view, this shift has a lot to do with perceptions of and attitudes toward refugees and migrants. Anti-refugee and anti-immigrant sentiments in the United States and in Europe stem from the perception that "migrants pose a socio-economic and ethno-cultural threat to western societies" (Chebel d'Appolonia 2012: 13). Immigrants are also regarded as threatening national identity and social cohesion. The current 'refugee crisis' in Europe has resulted in public discussions about the threat that Muslim refugees pose to the Christian identity of the continent. The debates are especially fervent in the new accession countries in Central Europe (Goździak and Márton 2018).

By the end of 2015, close to 400,000 mainly Muslim refugees and asylum seekers crossed the Serbian-Hungarian border and descended on the Keleti Railway Station in Budapest. Viktor Orbán, the Prime Minister of Hungary, did not see the arrival of refugees as a humanitarian challenge but as a Muslim invasion that required an appropriate security response: closing the Balkan land route to the European Union. A 100-mile-long, four-meter-high, razor-wire-topped fence on Hungary's southern borders with Serbia and Croatia was erected to keep refugees out. Hungarian border police, guns in holsters, swaggered in pairs alongside the fence in a scene reminiscent of the Cold War. Yet, somehow, this was not 'enough.' Hungary recruited 3,000 'border-hunters' to join the 10,000 police and soldiers already patrolling the border (Goździak 2016a), parts of which have recently been electrified. These actions stand in sharp contrast to the events of 1989, when Hungary opened its border with Austria and let thousands of East Germans through to West Germany (Haraszti 2015).

While it is true that the unprecedented arrival of refugees and asylum seekers in 2015 did result in a handful of jihadi terrorists entering the Schengen Zone through Hungary, the government has systematically used the arrival of refugees as an opportunity to stigmatize refugees as terrorists. Beyond political statements, armed military police patrols on the streets of Budapest, in metro stations and in public spaces, have become a regular sight, as is the case in Paris and Brussels, while Hungary has yet to experience a terrorist attack (Goździak and Márton 2018).

The final question I want to pose in this chapter is: Whom does the focus on migration and security help? Research indicates that it does not help trafficked migrants. 'Rescued' migrants are often sent back to the country that they wanted to escape (Sharma 2005). When they are allowed to stay in the destination country, the permission to stay rarely includes a long-term immigration relief with the accompanying rights that legal immigrants have. Many researchers emphasize the fact that the focus on crime and security overshadows the role of the state as a protector of human rights (see Ruggiero 1997; Kyle and Dale 2001; Anderson 2008). Does it help native-born citizens? My current research on norms and values and the 'refugee crisis' and my previous studies on attitudes toward migrants in Europe suggest that criminalizing migrants and migration fosters xenophobia, but doesn't necessarily prevent human trafficking, smuggling, and any other irregular migration.

References

Achilli, Luigi. 2017. *Human Smuggling Across the Mediterranean Sea*. Available: https://soundcloud.com/eib-institute-knowledge/luigi-achilli-human-smuggling-across-the-mediterranean-sea Accessed on June 22, 2018.

Adamson, Fiona B. 2006. Crossing Borders: International Migration and National Security. *International Security* 31 (1): 165–199.

Anderson, Bridget. 2008. "Illegal Immigrant": Victim or Villain? COMPAS Working Paper No 64.

Anderson, Sarah. 2013. The Connection Between Human Trafficking and Terrorism. Blog post available at: https://notenoughgood.com/2012/01/human-trafficking-and-terrorism/.

Anker, Christien, and van den and Ilse van Liempt. 2012. Human Rights and Migration. *Trafficking for Forced Labor*. Palgrave Macmillan.

Aronowitz, A.G.T., and E. Tyurykanova. 2010. *Analyzing the Business Model of Trafficking in Human Beings to Better Prevent the Crime*. Vienna: OSCE.

Barnett, Jon. 2003. Security and Climate Change. *Global Environmental Change* 13 (1): 7–17.

Bratich, Jack. 2006. Public Secrecy and Immanent Security. A Strategic Analysis. *Journal Cultural Studies* 20 (4–5): 493–511.

Bruckert, Christine, and Colltee Parent. 2002. *Trafficking in Human Beings and Organized Crime: A Literature Review*. Ottawa: Research and Evaluation Branch, Canadian Mounted Police.

Burgess, Peter J., Amicelle, Anthony, Bartels E.A.C., Bellanova, Rocco, Cerami, Alfio, Eggum, Erik, Hoogensen, Gunhild, Kittelsen, Sonja, Knibbe, K.E., de Koning, MJM, Koser, Khalid, Krause, Keith, and Salemink, OHJM. 2007. *Promoting Human Security: Ethical, Normative and Educational Frameworks in Western Europe*. UNESCO publications on Human Security, Peace and Conflict Prevention. Report.

Burnett, John, and Gonzales, Richard. 2018. John Kelly On Trump, The Russia Investigation and Separating Immigrant Families. NPR May 10. Available: https://www.npr.org/2018/05/10/609478998/john-kelly-despite-times-of-deep-frustration-no-regrets-taking-white-house-job Accessed on June 28, 2018.

Buzan, Barry, Ole Waever, and Jaap de Wilde. 1998. *Security: A New Framework for Analysis*. Boulder, CO: Rienner.

Caldwell, Bruce, Idrani Pieris, Caldwell Barkat-e-Khuda, John Caldwell, and Pat Caldwell. 1999. Sexual Regimes and Sexual Networking: The Risk of an HIV/AIDS Epidemic in Bangladesh. *Social Science and Medicine* 48 (8): 1103–1116.

Chipman, J. 1992. The Future of Strategic Studies: Beyond Grand Strategy. *Survival* 34: 109–131.

Chebel d'Appollonia, Ariane. 2012. *Frontiers of Fear. Immigration and Insecurity in the United States and Europe*. Ithaca: Cornell University Press.

Davidson, Thomas. 2005. Terrorism and Human Smuggling Rings in South and Central America. *Terrorism Monitor* 3 (22). Available at: https://jamestown.org/program/terrorism-and-human-smuggling-rings-in-south-and-central-america/.

Desyllas, Moshoula Capous. 2007. A Critique of the Global Trafficking Discourse and U.S. Policy. *The Journal of Sociology & Social Welfare* 34 (4): 57–80.

Dunai, Marton. 2019. Four Jailed for Life Over Death of 71 Migrants in Hungarian Truck. *Reuters*, June 20. Available at: https://www.reuters.com/article/us-europe-migrants-hungary-trial/four-jailed-for-life-over-death-of-71-in-austria-migrant-truck-idUSKCN1TL0LX.

Fischer, Robert J., Edward Halibozek, and G. Green. 2004. *Introduction to Security*. Boston, MA: Butterworth-Heinemann.

Gale, Sadie Levy. 2016. Refugee Crisis: Nearly 90,000 Unaccompanied Children Sought Asylum in Europe in 2015. *Independent*, May 3. Available at: https://www.independent.co.uk/news/world/nearly-90000-unaccompanied-minors-sought-asylum-in-eu-in-2015-a7010976.html

Gilardi, Jasper. 2020. Ally or Exploiter? The Smuggler-Migrant Relationship Is a Complex One. *Migration Information Source*, February 5. Available at: https://www.migrationpolicy.org/article/ally-or-exploiter-smuggler-migrant-relationship-complex-one

Goldstein, Daniel M. 2010. Toward a Critical Anthropology of Security. *Current Anthropology* 51 (4): 487–517.

Goldman, Emily O. 2001. New Threats, New Identities and New Ways of War: The Sources of Change in National Security Doctrine. *Journal of Strategic Studies* 24 (2): 43–76.

Gonzalez, Elsie. 2013. The Nexus between Human Trafficking and Terrorism/Organized Crime: Combating Human Trafficking By Creating a Cooperative Law Enforcement System. Law School Student Scholarship. Paper 227. Available at: https://scholarship.shu.edu/student_scholarship/227

Goździak E.M. 2015. *What kind of Welcome? Integration of Central American Children into local Communities*. Report prepared for the J.M. Kaplan Fund. Washington, DC: Institute for the Study of International Migration (ISIM).

Goździak, E.M. 2016a. Become a Border Hunter. Blog post.

Goździak E.M. 2016b. *Trafficked Children and Youth in the United States: Reimagining Survivors*. Rutgers University Press.
Goździak E.M., and P. Márton (2018). Where the Wild Things Are: Fear of Islam and the Anti-Refugee Rhetoric in Hungary and in Poland. Central and Eastern European Migration Review (online first): 1–27. doi: https://doi.org/10.17467/ceemr.2018.04.
Haraszti, Miklos. 2015. Behind Viktor Orbán's War on Refugees in Hungary. *New Perspectives Quarterly* 32 (4): 2–5.
Harding, Luke, and Daniel Nolan. 2015. Hungarian Police Make Arrests Over Lorry Containing 71 Bodies. *The Guardian*, August 29. Available at: https://www.theguardian.com/world/2015/aug/28/driver-of-lorry-containing-71-dead-refugees-is-arrested
Hathaway, James C. 2008. The Human Rights Quagmire of 'Human Trafficking'. *Virginia Journal of International Law* 49(1): 1–59.
Hay, James W., and Mark Andrejevic. 2006. Introduction: Toward an Analytic of Governmental Experiments in these Times: Homeland Security as the New Social Security. *Cultural Studies* 20 (4–5): 331–348. https://doi.org/10.1080/09502380600708747.
Haynes, Dina F. (2007). (Not) Found Chained to a Bed in a Brothel: Conceptual, Legal, and Procedural Failures to Fulfill the Promise of the Trafficking Victims Protection Act. *Georgetown Immigration Law Journal*, Available at SSRN: https://ssrn.com/abstract=984927.
Horsley, Scott. 2018. FACT CHECK: Trump, Illegal Immigration and Crime. Available: https://www.npr.org/2018/06/22/622540331/fact-check-trump-illegal-immigration-and-crime?t=1530190696085.Accessed June 28.
Juhasz, Judith. 2000. Migrant Trafficking and Human Smuggling in Hungary. In *Migrant Trafficking and Human Smuggling in Europe: A Review of Evidence with Case Studies from Hungary, Poland, and Ukraine*, ed. Frank Laczko and David Thompson, 167–232. Geneva: International Organization for Migration.
Keefer, Sandra L. 2006. *Human Trafficking and the Impact on National Security for the United States*. US Army War College.
Klare, Michael T., and Daniel C. Thomas, eds. 1994. *World Security: Challenges for a New Century*. New York: St. Martin's Press.
Koser, Khalid. 2011. When is Migration a Security Issue? Brookings 31.3. https://www.brookings.edu/opinions/when-is-migration-a-security-issue/.. Accessed on July 16.
Kyle, David, and John Dale. 2001. Smuggling the State Back in: Agents of Human Smugglings Reconsidered. In *Global Human Smuggling*, ed. Kyle and Ray Koslowski, 29–57. Baltimore: Johns Hopkins University Press.
Lee, Magee. 2011. *Trafficking and Global Crime Control*. London: Sage Publication.

Mahdavi, Parvis. 2014. *From Trafficking to Terror: Constructing a Global Social Problem*. Routledge.

Malarek, Victor. 2004. *The Natashas: Inside the New Global Sex Trade*. New York: Arcade Publishing.

McQuade, Aidan. 2015. The Lithuanian 'slaves' highlight the holes in Britain's anti-trafficking strategy. *The Guardian*, August 11, 2015.

Molland, Sverre. 2001. 'I am Helping Them': 'Traffickers', 'Anti-Traffickers' and Economies of Bad Faith. *The Australian Journal of Anthropology* 22: 236–254.

Mueller, John. 2006. *Overblown: How Politicians and the Terrorism Industry Inflate National Security Threats, and Why We Believe Them*, 272. Free Press.

Nickerson, James. 2016. Traffickers vs Smugglers: The Refugee Crisis is Changing How Migrants are Moved. *New Statesman*, May 12. Available at: https://www.newstatesman.com/world/europe/2016/05/traffickers-v-smugglers-refugee-crisis-changing-how-migrants-are-moved

Rana, Junaid. 2011. *Terrifying Muslims: Race, Labor and the South Asian Diaspora*. Durham, NC: Duke University Press.

Richards, Julian. 2012. *A Guide to National Security: Threats, Responses, and Strategies*. Oxford: Oxford University Press.

Ruggiero, Vincenzo. 1997. Criminals and Service Providers: Cross-National Dirty Economies. *Crime, Law and Social Change* 28: 27–38.

Salt, John. 2000. Trafficking and Human Smuggling: A European Perspective. *International Migration* 38 (3): 31–56.

Shannon, Sarah. 1999. Prostitution and the Mafia: The Involvement of Organized Crime in the Global Economy. In *Illegal Migration and Commercial Sex: The New Slave Trade*, ed. Phil Williams. London: Frank Cass.

Sharma, Nandita. 2005. Anti-Trafficking Rhetoric and the Making of a Global Aparthei. *NWSA Journal* 17(3): 88–111.

Shelly, Louise. 2010. *Human Trafficking: A Global Perspective*. Cambridge: Cambridge University Press.

Shoaps, Laura L. 2013. Room for Improvement: Palermo protocol and the Trafficking Victims Protection Act. *Lewis and Clark Law Review* 17 (3): 931–972.

Siddiqui, Sabrina. 2018. Trump's Travel Ban: What Does the Supreme Court Ruling Mean? *The Guardian*, June 27. Available: https://www.theguardian.com/us-news/2018/jun/26/trump-travel-ban-supreme-court-ruling-explained. Accessed June 28, 2018.

Soderlund, Gretchen. 2005. Running from the Rescuers: New U.S. Crusades against Sex Trafficking and the Rhetoric of Abolition. *NWSA Journal* 17(3): 64–87.

Stinson, Ainsley. 2012. The Securitization of Sex Trafficking: A Comparative Case Study of Sweden and the United States. B.A.H. (Sociology and International Development) Thesis, Dalhousie University.

Taibly, Rebecca. 2001. Organized Crime and People Smuggling/Trafficking in Australia. *Australian Institute of Criminology* 208: 1–6.

Tarry, Sarah. 2009. 'Deepening' and 'Widening': An Analysis of Security Definitions in the 1990s. *Journal of Military and Strategic Studies* 2 (1): 1–13.

UNODC. 2000. *Trafficking in Persons: Global Patterns*. UNODC.

Väyrynen, Raimo. 2003. Illegal Immigration, Human Trafficking, and Organized Crime, Discussion Paper No. 2003/72. Geneva: United Nations University.

Waever, Ole. 1996. European Security Identities. *Journal of Common Market Studies* 34 (1): 103–132.

Walker, R.B.J. 1990. Security, Sovereignty, and the Challenge of World Politics. *Alternatives: Global, Local, Political* 15(1): 3–27.

Weitzer, Ronald. 2005. Flawed Theory and Method in Studies of Prostitution. *Violence Against Women* 11 (7): 934–949.

Weitzer, Ronald. 2007. The Social Construction of Sex Trafficking: Ideology and Institutionalization of a Moral Crusade. *Politics and Society* 35 (3): 447–475.

Woodhouse, Leighton Akio. 2018. Trump's "Shithole Countries" Remark is at the Center of a Lawsuit to Reinstate Protections for Immigrants. Available: https://theintercept.com/2018/06/28/trump-tps-shithole-countries-lawsuit/.Accessed on June 28.

Wrever, O., Buzan, B., Kelstrup, M., Lemaitre, P., with Carlton, D., et al. 1993. *Identity, Migration and the New Security Agenda in Europe*. London: Pinter.

PART II

Fear of the Other

Since the terrorist attacks on the United States on September 11, 2001, new connections between crimes not normally associated with national security have been established. Human trafficking is one such crime. On December 16, 2002, President George W. Bush identified the correlation as more than a mere theoretical concern by signing National Security Directive 22, which specifically linked human trafficking to terrorist threats. More recent terrorist attacks in Paris, Brussels, and Nice have sparked similar assertions, despite the fact that the terrorists were French and Belgian citizens. Facts notwithstanding, policy-makers on both sides of the Atlantic allege that human smuggling and trafficking are a conduit for international terrorism. Increased international migration flows, growing multicultural populations, and the emergence of informal, migration-based, transnational networks that circulate capital, goods, and ideas challenge notions of the bounded state and call for greater policing of borders. In this section of the book, I focus on the Other–refugees and asylum seekers–perceived as a national security threat. In Chapter 4, I spotlight the US refugee resettlement program–its history, slow erosion, and the current danger of possible elimination—and argue that a robust refugee resettlement is not a threat but an asset of our national security. In Chapter 5, I focus on two European countries—Hungary and Poland–to showcase how human trafficking has replaced or been conflated with migration in public narratives, policy responses, and practice with refugees. I chose Hungary and Poland, two countries with virtually no refugees and immigrants, to illustrate the baseless fear of the Other that has led to erecting barbed wired fences, closing of borders and refugee camps, and shutting down the asylum system.

CHAPTER 4

Closing US Refugee Resettlement with the Stroke of a Pen

At the beginning of 2017, the newly elected 45th President of the United States signed several executive orders to "protect the nation from foreign terrorists entering the country" (Executive Order 13769 & 13780). The new administration feared that inadequate vetting of refugees to be resettled in the United States and issuing visas to citizens of Muslim-majority countries would threaten the security of the American society and result in another terrorist attack.

Two years later, in the summer of 2019, reports started circulating that some officials in the Trump administration had proposed resettling zero refugees in Fiscal Year 2020 (Jenkins 2019). As we learnt at the beginning of October 2020, the administration did not totally close the refugee resettlement program, but got very close to it by capping the refugee admission ceiling at 18,000 individuals (Nakamura et al. 2019). This decision came at a time when an unprecedented 70.8 million people around the world have been forced from home. Among them are nearly 26 million refugees, over half of whom are under 18 years of age (UNHCR 2019). According to experts, 1.4 million refugees are in need of resettlement globally (RCUSA 2019). Following the administration's attempts to bar access to asylum, any further decimation—or worse, elimination—of the refugee resettlement program in FY2020 would amount to a total refugee ban.

E. M. Goździak, *Human Trafficking as a New (In)Security Threat*,
https://doi.org/10.1007/978-3-030-62873-4_4

In this chapter, I debate the effects of the executive orders indefinitely barring Syrian refugees from entering the United States, suspending all refugee admissions for 120 days, and blocking citizens of several Muslim-majority countries from entering the United States for 90 days. I also analyze the effects of the drastic cuts in refugee admissions on the humanitarian nature of the US refugee resettlement program, the safety and security of Muslim refugees and immigrants living in the country, and the national security of the country. I begin with a brief history of the US refugee resettlement to showcase its beginnings, its peaks, slow erosion, and the current danger of possible elimination. I argue—and I am not alone—that a robust refugee resettlement program is indeed crucial to our national security.

US Refugee Resettlement Program in a Snapshot

The modern history of refuge in the United States goes back to the Displaced Persons Act of 1948, which many consider the beginning of the US refugee resettlement program (Haines 2010). This does not mean that those fleeing persecution did not seek refuge in the country before 1948. Of course, many did. Some successfully, others not. Probably, the most infamous rejection of refugees trying to enter the United States is represented by the ill-fated voyage of the St. Louis, carrying onboard over 900 mostly German Jews fleeing the Nazi regime in 1939 (Ogilive and Miller 2006). In the same year, an attempt to allow 20,000 German Jewish refugee children was also rebuffed. These two incidences are textbook examples of prejudice and anti-Semitism.

In contrast to widespread public and political indifference toward refugees before World War II, the situation changed after the war. In 1945, President Harry Truman went behind the backs of an anti-immigrant Congress and xenophobic country and issued *The Truman Directive*. Twenty-three thousand unwanted Jewish refugees entered America in 1946 under his executive order. Three years later, following constant pressure from the White House, Congress finally passed the Displaced Persons Act of 1948. As welcome as this legislation was, it fell short of its more inclusive aims.

The Displaced Persons Act authorized admissions of refugees from Europe and permitted asylum seekers already in the United States to regularize their status. This limited term bill provided for admission of 200,000 displaced persons and attempted to favor Catholic and Protestant refugees over Jewish ones by enacting preferences for agricultural workers. Although Asians received no refugee visas, the Act enabled several thousand Chinese already residing in the United States to gain legal permanent status by claiming asylum. Many were highly educated and well connected, with skills and knowledge considered strategic for the United States, and worth keeping away from the communist side (Bockley 1995). The Displaced Persons Act expired at the end of 1952.

On August 7, 1953, President Dwight D. Eisenhower signed into law the Refugee Relief Act to supplant the Displaced Persons Act. The new legislation resulted in the admission of 214,000 immigrants to the United States, including 60,000 Italians, 17,000 Greeks, 17,000 Dutch, and 45,000 men, women, and children from countries under communist control. Upon signing the new law, Eisenhower said: "In enacting this legislation, we are giving a new chance in life to 214,000 fellow humans. This action demonstrates again America's traditional concern for the homeless, the persecuted, and the less fortunate of other lands. It is a dramatic contrast to the tragic events taking place in East Germany and in other captive nations" (quoted in Glass 2018, no page number).

Not everybody was as enthusiastic as President Eisenhower about the new law. Sen. Pat McCarran (D-Nev) argued that amendments that required applicants to undergo an in-depth security screening should be added. In seeking to block increased immigration, McCarran argued that many immigrants already in the United States are not well integrated, emphasizing lack of capacity to resettle the "untold millions (...) storming our gates for admission and those gates are cracking under the strain," and underscoring security concerns with alarming pronouncements that those admitted under the new law will "promote this Nation's downfall [more] than any other group since we achieved our independence as a nation" (quoted in Glass 2018).

A few years later, the same desire to protect refugees escaping a communist regime governed the resettlement of Hungarians fleeing the Soviet repression of the 1956 Hungarian Revolution. Some 200,000 Hungarians fled the country as Soviet tanks rolled into Budapest to crush, once and for all, a national uprising. Most fled to nearby Austria (Zieck 2013), but the United States brought in 38,000 Hungarians within the span of three months (Pastor 2016). The Hungarian resettlement process represented a novel approach to immigration policy. Instead of the legislative branch, it was the White House that took charge of the effort (Bon Tempo 2008).

On November 8, 1956, the US government announced that 5,000 'escapee visas' would be made available for the Hungarian refugees per the Refugee Relief Act of 1953, which was about the expire at the end of December. Over 6,000 Hungarians were admitted with escapee visas. The rest entered under the parole provision of the Immigration and Nationality Act, also known as the McCarran-Walter Act (see Markowitz 1973; Bursten 1958). Originally, the parolees were allowed to live and work in the United States, but were not given a formal immigrant status until July 1958, through legislative action, when it became clear that they would not return to Hungary any time soon (Markowitz 1973).

Twenty-seven years after the Displaced Persons Act of 1948, in response to the large numbers of refugees created by the Vietnam War, the Indochina Migration and Refugee Assistance Act of 1975 created a domestic resettlement program for Vietnamese and Cambodian refugees. Laotians were made eligible for the program a year later, in 1976. However, it was not until 1980, that a full-fledged refugee resettlement program was created. The Refugee Act of 1980 established a domestic resettlement program for all refugees. It defined 'refugee' in accordance with the 1967 United Nations Protocol on Refugees as a person with well-founded fear of persecution for reasons of race, religion, nationality, membership in a particular social group or political opinion, and removed refugees from the immigration preference system (Ewing 2012).

The Refugee Act of 1980 established a formal US refugee resettlement system with a network of agencies that have formed a public-private partnership with the US government, including the US State Department for the admission of refugees and initial reception and placement services and with the US Office of Refugee Resettlement (ORR) for continued services. Prior to 2017, the network included 325 local agencies serving refugees in every state of the Union except Wyoming (RCUSA 2019a)

The Refugee Act also established that the president, in consultation with Congress, is responsible for setting the number of refugees to be admitted to the country each fiscal year. The United States has historically led the world in refugee resettlement. Between 1980 and 2018, the United States has resettled three million of the more than four million refugees resettled worldwide (Connor and Krogstad 2018), admitting on average 80,000 refugees annually, with as many as 200,000 a year in the early 1980s (UNHCR 2019a).

For 40 years, the US refugee resettlement program enjoyed bipartisan support from Congress and six successive US presidents. Congress continues to provide bipartisan support to the refugee resettlement program as evidenced by the recent revival of the bipartisan Refugee

Caucus in the US House of Representatives (RCUSA 2019a). In 2018, members of the Refugee Caucus urged the president to maintain the US Refugee Admissions Program and for the administration to set a level for accepting refugees that "will continue to align with global need and signal to the international community that the US will continue to be a global leader in refugee protection" (Harding 2018). A year later, it seems that this call to action has fallen on deaf ears.

Before I discuss the current administration's attempts to *de facto* shut down the refugee resettlement program, it is prudent to mention other factors that have contributed to the slow erosion of the program aimed at protecting and ensuring security of refugees and asylum seekers. I have to mention, however briefly, the chilling effects of the terrorist attacks on the United States on September 11, 2001 on refugee admissions. It is also worth bringing up 'expedited removal,' a provision stemming from the Illegal Immigration Reform and Immigrant Responsibility Act (IRIRA) of 1996 and the continued erosion of the Temporary Protected Status (TPS).

The Chilling Effect of 9/11 on Refugee Admissions

Only once in the history of the US refugee resettlement was the program shut down. Two weeks after the terrorist attacks on September 11, 2001, a plane full of Afghan refugees arrived at John F. Kennedy Airport (JFK). Many such planes landed at JFK before 9/11. However, this time airport officials alerted Mayor Giuliani's office and stated that hundreds of Afghans had just landed in New York City. Alarmed, the Mayor called Vice President Dick Cheney and within days the US refugee resettlement program, the first refugee protection casualty of the terrorist attacks, was shut down. The vice president and other American officials perceived resettlement as being particularly vulnerable to security problems. They contended that the refugee and asylum programs could be exploited by terrorist networks (see Kerwin 2005; Leiken 2004). The arrest in May 2011 of two Iraqi refugees in Kentucky for conspiring to provide weapons to Al-Qaeda indicates that some vulnerabilities persist (Richey 2011). Nonetheless, the chance of being killed on US soil in a terrorist attack committed by a refugee was 1 in 3.86 billion a year. "In fact," writes Alex Nowrasteh in an extensive analysis of terrorists by immigration status, "the annual chance of being murdered by someone other than a foreign-born terrorist in a normal homicide was 264 times greater than the chance of dying in a foreign-born terrorist's attack" (Nowrasteh 2019: 2).

The total shut down of the program was brief—three months—while security measures were examined. But three years later the program was still operating at only about two-thirds of its previous capacity. As Andrew Schoenholtz (2005: 324) wrote, "more than 100,000 refugees have lost opportunities to build new lives in the United States during this period." Despite the sharp decline in refugee resettlement in the immediate period following 9/11, the United States managed to resettle more refugees (33,000) than any other one country during that time (Kerwin 2018). Following the United States were Canada (27,000), Australia (15,000), and the United Kingdom (6,000). Sweden, Germany, Norway, and France each resettled about 3,000 refugees (Connor and Krogstad 2018). The refugee admissions had rebounded to nearly 75,000 per year by fiscal years 2009 and 2010, before falling below 75,000 in fiscal year 2011 (Kerwin 2012). The Obama administration's goal was to admit 110,000 refugees in fiscal year 2017, which would have been the highest number since 1994. In the last year of the Obama administration, the United States resettled close to 85,000 refugees, a few thousand short of the original goal (Krogstad and Radford 2017).

The Faltering US Protection for Refugees and Asylum Seekers

For many years, the United States has also granted political asylum to more than 20,000 persons each year, extended temporary protected status (TPS) to tens of thousands of foreign nationals fearing return to their home countries because of armed conflict, egregious abuses of human rights, or natural disasters, and offered protection to survivors of human trafficking. However, despite its generosity, the US refugee protection system has been eroding in recent years (Kerwin 2012).

Post-9/11 security measures, combined with US interdiction policies, have prevented many asylum seekers from reaching safe haven in the United States. The 'expedited removal' process, a procedure, created in 1996 by the Illegal Immigration Reform and Immigration Responsibility Act (IRAIRA), that allows US Customs and Border Protection (CBP) officials to rapidly deport non-citizens who are undocumented or who have committed misrepresentation or fraud, has expanded considerably over the years. In order to avoid summary removal, migrants must express a fear of persecution or request political asylum to an immigration officer. If they ask for political asylum, they are supposed to be interviewed by an asylum officer from the US Citizenship and Immigration Service (USCIS). The goal of this interview is to determine whether they indeed have a 'credible fear' of persecution (INA 1996). During the "credible fear" process, they must be detained (see Kerwin 2012, 2016). However, the US Commission on International Religious Freedom (USCIRF) found that in one of every six cases in which migrants expressed a fear of return they did not receive 'credible fear' interviews and were removed in contravention of the law.

The most recent expansion of the expedited removal happened on July 23, 2019, when the Department of Homeland Security (DHS) announced that most undocumented persons who cannot prove they have resided in the United States for more than two years will be subject to expedited removal (Benenson 2019). Immigration advocates, including the National Immigration Law Center and the US Commission on International Religious Freedom, among others, plan to challenge this expansion in court. Immigrant rights advocates have previously expressed concerns about the lack of due process involved in expedited removal, both at designated ports of entry and for people in the border zone (Caplan-Bricker 2014). The American Civil Liberties Union has argued that expedited removal can lead to the deportation of many people who would qualify for asylum (ACLU 2015a). The ACLU has also noted that the 100-mile "border zone" within which expedited removal can be carried out houses roughly two-thirds of the US population, and has expressed concern about the implications of these broad enforcement powers for civil rights and constitutional protections (ACLU 2015b). The Immigration Policy Council noted that expedited removal proceedings and other rapid deportation decisions "often fail to take into account many critical factors, including whether the individual is eligible to apply for lawful status in the United States, whether he or she has long-standing ties here, or whether he or she has US-citizen family members" (Immigration Policy Council 2014).

Speaking about the administration making asylum seekers wait in Mexico, Michael Knowles, president of the union that represents hundreds of asylum officers and other immigration workers, said:

> One of our concerns is that those immigration agents do not even ask the individual if they're afraid to remain in Mexico. It's only if the applicant affirmatively says on their own 'Oh, but I'm afraid to go back to Mexico.' That's when they would be referred to an asylum officer. We have had cases where officers and their supervisors believe strongly that the individual met the high standard but they were overturned by higher ups at headquarters. (Scamisso 2019)

In 2015, the US House of Representatives voted 289–137 to pass the American Security Against Foreign Enemies Act of 2015, also known as the SAFE Act (Ayoub and Rondon 2017). The SAFE Act specifically singled out refugees coming from Syria or Iraq. The Act was created in response to the November 2015 Paris attacks, out of concern that ISIL terrorists would enter the United States posing as refugees fleeing Syria (Al Jazeera 2015). The attacks have turned possible admission of refugees fleeing war-torn Syria and Iraq into a high-stakes political issue.

The Act was met with many criticisms. Democrats opposing the Republican bill said the United States has no business abandoning its age-old values, including being a safe haven for people fleeing countries racked by violence. The then FBI Director, James Comey, said the SAFE Act "seeks to micromanage the process in a way that is counter-productive to national security, to our humanitarian obligation, and the overall ability to focus on Homeland Security" (cited in Perez 2015). At the same time, the Vice President of the European Commission, Federica Mogherini, pointed out that the Paris attackers were EU citizens, not Syrian refugees: "It is all EU citizens so far. This can change with the hours, but so far it is quite clear it is an issue of internal domestic security" (cited in Porter 2015). The American Civil Liberties Union (ACLU) called the measure "un-American" and said it would bring US resettlement of refugees to a grinding halt, rather than a "pause" as the bill's supporters asserted. The US Holocaust Memorial Museum weighed in on the discussions and said it "looks with concern upon the current refugee crisis" and drew a comparison between Syrian refugees unable to enter the United States and "Jews who were unable to flee Nazism" (Al Jazeera 2015).

Conflating refugees with terrorists, imagining that traffickers infiltrate refugee populations and place terrorists among them, made Donald Trump, in his first year in the office, lower the refugee admission cap from 110,000 to 45,000. He later reduced the cap to 30,000 people and most recently set it at 18,000 individuals—the lowest in the history of the refugee resettlement program.

On January 27, 2017, Donald Trump signed Executive Order 13769 entitled Protecting the Nation from Foreign Terrorist Entry into the United States. The order denied for 120 days the entry of refugees and banned for 90 days the entry into the United States of individuals from seven predominantly Muslim countries: Iran, Iraq, Libya, Somalia, Sudan, Syria, and Yemen. Many criticized the executive order: Democratic and Republican members of Congress, universities, business leaders, major corporations, Catholic bishops, and Jewish organizations. Some 1,000 US diplomats signed a dissent cable opposing the order, setting a record (Schwartz 2017). Public opinion was divided, with initial national polls yielding inconsistent results, from 57% of the polled respondents favoring the ban (Rasmussen poll) to the same percentage opposing it (Gallup poll), and others being split (Reuters). The inconsistencies stemmed from the questions asked in the polls. The Rasmussen poll asked whether people favored a temporary ban from seven countries until the government improves its screening for potential terrorists; the Reuters poll asked whether people agreed or disagreed with an order signed by Trump blocking refugees and banning people from seven Muslim-majority countries; and the Gallup poll asked whether people approved of Trump ordering a temporary ban for most people from seven predominantly Muslim countries (Bump 2017).

The ban resulted in the removal of some arriving non-immigrants and the revocation of more than 60,000 visas. Thousands of protesters gathered at airports across the country on the Sunday following the signing of the executive order. The ban, which took effect immediately upon its signing, caused sudden chaos at US airports and resulted in the removal of some arriving nonimmigrants and the revocation of more than 60,000 visas (Chishti et al. 2018). Dulles airport serving the Washington, DC, area was a place of tense scenes among protesters, Democratic congressmen, and transit officials. Among those detained at airports were numerous US permanent residents; in some cases, they were held for up to 30 hrs despite the fact that the White House Chief of Staff indicated that green card holders were exempted from the executive order (Gambino et al 2017).

The order quickly became subject to multiple legal challenges. The Muslim American Society was one of the organizations challenging the order. Several federal courts temporarily restrained or enjoined parts of the executive order. In order to avoid these legal pitfalls, the order has been revised several times over the next year and a half. Executive Order 13780, with the same title, was signed on March 6, 2017. The new order delayed the implementation date and exempted individuals who were previously authorized to travel to the United States. The day before the new order was to take effect, it became subject to a nationwide temporary restraining order. However, the Supreme Court later allowed for partial implementation with respect to foreigners without a *bona fide* relationship with a US-based individual or entity indicating that the administration was successful in avoiding legal challenges. The Supreme Court's decision has given some Transportation Security Administration and Customs & Border Control officers the liberty to discriminate against Muslims, detaining them or putting them through unwarranted secondary screening at ports of entry around the United States.

The Muslim American Society asserted that:

> (…) this ban despite its premise has no basis in ensuring the safety of the nation as no foreign nationals of any of these countries have perpetrated any acts of terror on US soil. Weighing the attitudes and statements of bigotry by the President on his campaign trail and further since assuming office, there is no doubt that this ban proves a legitimate first step in legalizing anti-Muslim bigotry by the US government. This is a very dangerous step not only for the United States but also for the rest of the world as the politics of Washington have far reaching global consequences.

The executive orders paved the way for further erosion of the refugee resettlement program. In addition to lowering the cap on the number of admitted refugees by 40 percent in just one year, the current administration has also allowed local jurisdictions more leeway in rejecting refugees who are being resettled across the country. Some experts assert that such powers are less relevant at a time when very few refugees are being admitted (Nakamura et al. 2019). I wonder, however, how this new power given to states and localities might affect refugees already resettled in the United States. Will discrimination against refugees increase? Will violence follow?

In a recent opinion piece published in *The Washington Post*, former Vice President Walter Mondale (2019) recalls a day some 40 years ago when he stood before the Geneva Meeting on Refugees and Displaced Persons in Southeast Asia at a time when hundreds of thousands of women, men, and children fled the south of Vietnam. The conference Mondale was addressing, convened by the United Nations, was a wake-up call meant to draw the attention of the world to a horrific humanitarian crisis. Following the conference, the US Refugee Act of 1980 was signed into law by President Jimmy Carter. The act received full bipartisan support in the Senate before President Carter signed it. The act tripled the number of refugees the United States would admit, and, most importantly, amended the definition of refugee to include someone with "well-founded fear of persecution." In his op-ed, Walter Mondale bemoans the fact that Donald Trump "has twisted the perception of refugees and asylum seekers into an unrecognizable lie. But here are the facts: Asylum seekers and refugees leave their countries because they have no choice — for many, if they stay, they will be persecuted, subjected to traumatic events such as torture, or killed." Mondale reminds us that refugees and asylum seekers have the legal right to seek protection from persecution.

This includes the asylum seekers at the US southern border with Mexico. However, the current administration considers all asylum seekers traveling through Mexico by land to the southern border ineligible for asylum if they have not first sought protection there before reaching the United States. Hundreds of thousands of Central Americans and others have been affected by the restrictions that took effect in July 2019 (Aleaziz 2019). This policy has enraged many refugee and migration advocates, but it has also angered asylum officers. The labor union which represents them has filed a fourth amicus brief since January 2017 in the 9th Circuit Court of Appeals in opposition to the administration's cruel and harmful asylum policies (Allyn 2019). In June 2020, the Trump administration proposed a new asylum law that would make it virtually impossible for many people, including women and children, fleeing gang and domestic violence to obtain asylum in the United States (Giovagnoli 2020).

The question remains: Is refugee protection incompatible with national security?

Refugee Protection and National Security: Complementary, Not Competing Imperatives

On September 3, 2019, over 20 retired General and Flag Officers of the US military sent a letter to Donald Trump expressing their concerns about the state of the US refugee resettlement program. In the letter, they wrote:

> For decades, the refugee resettlement program provided life-saving assistance, demonstrated our humanitarian leadership and values, supported allies hosting the vast majority of refugees, and served critical national security interests.

Indeed, top military officers have indicated that a robust refugee resettlement program serves national security interests. It does not jeopardize the safety of the nation.

Donald Kerwin (2016), a legal migration scholar, emphasizes the same point and indicates that refugee protection and national security are inextricably linked needs. "Refugee protection arises from an ethic of solidarity rooted in a belief in human dignity and equality," writes Kerwin (2016: 91). Interpreted broadly, national security refers to more than national defense, strong military, secure borders, and absence of wars. It refers to the protection of "a people, territory and way of life" (Jordan et al. 2009: 3–4). National security also aims at preserving a nation's "values, principles, and way of life" (DHS 2010: v).

Rather than being perceived as a threat, robust refugee protection system can positively influence three "core areas of state power: economic, military and diplomatic" (Adamson 2006: 185). As David Martin writes (2009), in a globalized world, economic prosperity of one nation is not possible without contact with the rest of the world. Refugees contribute to the economic prosperity of resettlement countries where they pay taxes and origin countries through remittances (see Chamie 2013; Clemens et al. 2008; UNGA 2013).

Refugee protection and legal refugee admission policies go a long way toward furthering the rule of law by preventing human trafficking, limiting migrant smuggling (Ginsburg 2010), and disrupting possible linkages between irregular migration and terrorism (Schmid 2016). Additionally, the US refugee resettlement program has had an illustrious history of supporting our foreign policy agenda, including protection of

Soviet Jews and other religious minorities. The United States participated in the 1989 Comprehensive Plan of Action (CPA), a unique international cooperation to address 'burden-sharing' in the aftermath of the Vietnam War between host countries of first asylum, the country of origin, and third countries beyond the region which pledged to resettle a certain number of refugees. The CPA promoted stability of allied states that hosted large refugee populations in Southeast Asia (Betts 2006).

In the United States, refugees have served as a continuous reminder of the nation's core values, including its commitment to religious liberty. As the Obama administration recognized, US success in promoting security and values abroad turns on its adherence to its values "at home" (White House 2015: 19). Sadly, these values do not seem to matter to the current administration (and many other populist governments around the world). Today's refugees and asylum seekers are thought not to be compatible with the 'America First' sentiments.

The closing sentences of Walter Mondale's recent op-ed piece seem to be appropriate to close this chapter: "When enough voices are raised, change can happen. As we promised in Geneva, it is time to take action: History will not forgive us if we fail. History will not forget us if we succeed" (Mondale 2019).

References

ACLU. 2015a. ACLU Comments on INS Notice to Expand Expedited Removal. American Civil Liberties Union. Available at: https://www.aclu.org/other/aclu-comments-ins-notice-expand-expedited-removal.

ACLU. 2015b. Know Your Rights: The Government's 100-Mile "Border" Zone—Map. American Civil Liberties Union. Available at: https://www.aclu.org/know-your-rights/border-zone/.

Adamson, Fiona. 2006. Crossing Borders: International Migration and National Security. *International Security* 31(1): 165–99. Available at: https://www.mitpressjournals.org/doi/10.1162/isec.2006.31.1.165.

Aleazis, Hamed. 2019. Asylum Officers Are Urging A Court To Strike Down Trump's Asylum Ban And Saying It "Rips At The Moral Fabric Of Our Country." BuzzFeed.news October 14. Available at: https://www.buzzfeednews.com/article/hamedaleaziz/asylum-officers-urge-ban-block-court-border-law?fbclid=IwAR3Epdi8CXWJETVQPNMQv3sOUepGNQ_24bA-Rlm4n4_MmvabqWiN4HrXN8U.

Al Jazeera. 2015. House Votes to Curb Syrian Refugees, Snubs Obama Veto Threat. Available at: http://america.aljazeera.com/articles/2015/11/19/house-votes-to-curb-syrian-refugees.html.

Allyn, Bobby. 2019. Asylum Officers: Trump's 'Remain In Mexico' Policy Is Against 'Moral Fabric' of US. National Public Radio June 27. Available at: https://www.npr.org/2019/06/27/736461700/asylum-officers-trumps-remain-in-mexico-policy-is-against-moral-fabric-of-u-s.

Ayoub, Abed A., and Rondon, Yolanda C. 2017. Willful Blindness or Deliberate Indifference: The United States' Abdication of Legal Responsibility to Refugees. *Barry Law Review* 22(1): 47–63. Available at: http://lawpublications.barry.edu/barrylrev/vol22/iss1/3.

Benenson, Lawrence. 2019. Expanded Expedited Removal. Washington, DC: National Immigration Forum. Available at: https://immigrationforum.org/article/expanded-expedited-removal/.

Betts, Alexander. 2006. Comprehensive Plans of Action: Insights from CIREFCA and the Indochinese CPA. New Issues in Refugee Research. Working Paper No. 120. Available at: https://www.unhcr.org/43eb6a152.pdf.

Bockley, Kathryn M. 1995. A Historical Overview of Refugee Legislation: The Deception of Foreign Policy in the Land of Promise. *North Carolina Journal of International Law and Commercial Regulation* 21(1): 253–292.

Bon Tempo, Carl J. 2008. *Americans at the Gate: The United States and Refugees During the Cold War*. Princeton: Princeton University Press.

Bronee, Sten A. 1993. The History of the Comprehensive Plan of Action. *International Journal of Refugee Law* 5(4): 534–543. Available at https://doi.org/10.1093/ijrl/5.4.534.

Bump, Philip. 2017. Do Americans Support Trump's Immigration Action? Depends on Who's Asking, and How. *Washington Post* February 2.

Bursten, Martin A. 1958. *Escape from Fear*. Syracuse: Syracuse University Press.

Caplan-Bricker, Nora. 2014. Deported Without Seeing A Judge: One of the Worst Parts of the Immigration System. *The New Republic*, April 14. Available at: https://newrepublic.com/article/117355/expedited-removal-deportations-immigrants-dont-get-due-process.

Chamie, Joseph. 2013. "The Choice: More Immigrants or Fewer Citizens?" Yale Global, March 4.

Chishti, Muzaffar, Sarah Pierce, and Laura Plata. 2018. In Upholding Travel Ban, Supreme Court Endorses Presidential Authority While Leaving Door Open for Future Challenges. *Migration Information Source*. June 29. Washington, DC: Migration Policy Institute. Available at: https://www.migrationpolicy.org/article/upholding-travel-ban-supreme-court-endorses-presidential-authority-while-leaving-door-open.

Clemens, Michael, Claudio E. Montenegro, and Lant Pritchett. 2008. The Place Premium: Wage Differences for Identical Workers across the US Border—Working Paper 148. Washington, DC: Center for Global Development.

Connor, Phillip and Krogstad, Jens Manuel. 2018. For the First Time, US Resettles Fewer Refugees than the Rest of the World. Washington, DC: Pew Research Center. Available at: https://www.pewresearch.org/fact-tank/2018/07/05/for-the-first-time-u-s-resettles-fewer-refugees-than-the-rest-of-the-world/.

DHS (US Department of Homeland Security). 2010. Quadrennial Homeland Security Review Report: A Strategic Framework for a Secure Homeland. Washington, DC: DHS. Available at: https://www.dhs.gov/sites/default/files/publications/2010-qhsr-report.pdf.

Ewing, Walter A. 2012. *Opportunity and Exclusion: A Brief History of US Immigration Policy*. Washington, DC: Immigration Policy Council. Available at: https://americanimmigrationcouncil.org/sites/default/files/research/opportunity_exclusion_011312.pdf.

Executive Order Protecting the Nation From Foreign Terrorist Entry Into The United States. E.O. 13780 of March 6, 2017. Available at: https://www.federalregister.gov/documents/2017/03/09/2017–04837/protecting-the-nation-from-foreign-terrorist-entry-into-the-united-states.

Executive Order Protecting the Nation From Foreign Terrorist Entry Into The United States. E.O. 13769 of January 27, 2017. Available at: https://www.federalregister.gov/documents/2017/02/01/2017-02281/protecting-the-nation-from-foreign-terrorist-entry-into-the-united-states.

Gambino, Lauren, Sabrina Siddiqui, Paul Owen, and Edward Helmore. 2017. Thousands protest against Trump travel ban in cities and airports nationwide. *The Guardian* January 30.

Ginsburg, Susan. 2010. *Securing Human Mobility in the Age of Risk: New Challenges for Travel, Migration, and Borders*. Washington, DC: Migration Policy Institute.

Giovagnoli, Mary. 2020. Trump's Anti-Asylum Rule Spells Disaster for Women and Girls. Ms. Magazine July 8. Available at: https://msmagazine.com/2020/07/08/trumps-anti-asylum-rule-spells-disaster-for-women-and-girls/.

Glass, Andrew. 2018. Eisenhower signs Refugee Relief Act, August 7, 1953. *Politico* August 7, 2018.

Haines, David W. 2010. *Safe Haven?: A History of Refugees in America*. Sterling, VA: Kumarian Press.

Harding, Robert. 2018. Katko, bipartisan House Caucus to Trump: Don't Cut Refugee Cap. Available at: https://auburnpub.com/blogs/eye_on_ny/katko-bipartisan-house-caucus-to-trump-don-t-cut-refugee/article_0519b204-bc1b-11e8-bfec-937dff5eb2af.html.

Immigration Policy Council. 2014. Removal Without Recourse: The Growth of Summary Deportations from the United States. Immigration Policy Council. April 28. Available at: https://www.americanimmigrationcouncil.org/research/removal-without-recourse-growth-summary-deportations-united-states.

Jenkins, Jack. 2019. Faith Groups Fear the End of Refugee Resettlement in the US. *Religion News Service*. July 22. Available at: https://religionnews.com/2019/07/19/faith-groups-fear-the-end-of-refugee-resettlement-in-the-u-s/.

Jordan, Amos A., William J. Taylor, Jr., Michael J. Meese, and Suzanne C. Nielsen. 2009. *American National Security*, 6th Ed. Baltimore and London: The Johns Hopkins University Press.

Kerwin, Donald. 2005. The Use and Misuse of 'National Security' Rationale in Crafting US Refugee and Immigration Policies. *International Journal of Refugee Protection* 17: 749–763.

Kerwin, Donald. 2012. The Faltering US Refugee Protection System: Legal and Policy responses to Refugees, Asylum-Seekers, and Others in Need of protection. *Refugee Survey Quarterly* 31 (1):1–33.

Kerwin, Donald. 2016. How Robust Refugee Protection Policies Can Strengthen Human and National Security. *Journal of Migration and Human Security* 4 (3): 83–140.

Kerwin, Donald. 2018. The US Refugee Resettlement Program—A Return to First Principles: How Refugees Help to Define, Strengthen, and Revitalize the United States. *Journal on Migration and Human Security* 6 (3): 205–225.

Krogstad, Jens Manuel, and Radford, Jynnah. 2017. Key Facts about Refugees to the US. Washington, DC: Pew Research Center. Available at: https://www.pewresearch.org/fact-tank/2017/01/30/key-facts-about-refugees-to-the-u-s/.

Leiken, Robert S. 2004. The Bearers of Global Jihad?: Immigration and National Security after 9/11, Research Paper, Washington, D.C., The Nixon Center. Available at: http://www.mafhoum.com/press7/193S23.pdf.

Markowitz, Arthur A. 1973. Humanitarianism versus Restrictionism: The United States and the Hungarian Refugees. *International Migration Review* 7 (1): 46–59.

Martin, David. 2009. Refining Immigration Law's Role in Counterterrorism. Series on Counterterrorism and American Statutory Law, a joint project of the Brookings Institution, the Georgetown University Law Center, and the Hoover Institution. Washington, DC: Brookings Institution. Available at: https://www.brookings.edu/wp-content/uploads/2016/06/0310_immigration_martin.pdf.

Mondale, Walter. 2019. We are Once Again in a Humanitarian Refugee Crisis. We Must Stem this Misery. *Washington Post* July 23. Available at: https://beta.washingtonpost.com/opinions/walter-mondale-america-has-saved-thousands-of-refugees-we-must-again/2019/07/23/b629e6de-aa47-11e9-86dd-d7f0e60391e9_story.html.

Nakamura, David, Maria Sacchetti, and Seung Min Kim. 2019. Trump Administration Slashes Refugee Limit for the Third Consecutive Year to a Historic Low of 18,000. *Washington Post*, September 27.

Nowrasteh, Alex. 2019. Terrorists by Immigration Status and Nationality: A Risk Analysis, 1975–2017. *Policy Analysis*. Cato Institute. Available at: https://www.cato.org/sites/cato.org/files/pubs/pdf/pa_866_edit.pdf.

Ogilive, Sarah A., and Miller, Scott. 2006. *Refuge Denied. The St. Louis Passengers and the Holocaust*. Madison, WI: University of Wisconsin Press.

Pastor, Peter. 2016. The American Reception and Settlement of Hungarian Refugees in 1956–1957. Hungarian Cultural Studies. *e-Journal of the American Hungarian Educators Association* 9.

Perez, Evan. 2015. First on CNN: FBI Director James Comey Balks at Refugee Legislation. Available at: https://edition.cnn.com/2015/11/19/politics/fbi-director-james-comey-refugee-legislation/index.html.

Porter, Tom. 2015. Paris Attacks: Police Arrest Man Carrying Same Passport as One Found Near Suicide Bomber. International Business Times November 17. Available at: https://www.ibtimes.co.uk/paris-attacks-police-arrest-man-carrying-same-passport-one-found-near-suicide-bomber-1529087.

RCUSA. 2019. *No Justification: The Administration's Crusade To Ban All Refugees*. July 18. Available at: http://www.rcusa.org/blog.

RCUSA. 2019a. Where are the Refugees? Drastic Cuts to Refugee Resettlement Harming Refugees, Communities and American leadership. Washington, DC. Available at: http://www.rcusa.org/rcusa-report-2019.

Richey, Warren. 2011. Iraqi Refugees in Kentucky Charged with Planning to Help Arm Al Qaeda. *Christian Science Monitor* 31 May. Available at: https://www.csmonitor.com/USA/Justice/2011/0531/Iraqi-refugees-in-Kentucky-charged-with-planning-to-help-arm-Al-Qaeda.

Scamisso, Ben. 2019. The US is Forcing Thousands of Asylum Seekers to Wait in Dangerous Border Towns with Little Help from Mexico—And none from the US. Newsy.com October 3. Available at: https://www.newsy.com/stories/the-us-is-keeping-at-risk-migrants-in-mexico-without-aid/?fbclid=IwAR0rHCfoxjkcc2b4MZ8C8oXWhGNGSgfie7FW1E5QPb1qb3Iidh4GR3Mwug0.

Schmid, Alex P. 2016. Links between Terrorism and Migration: An Exploration. The International Centre for Counter-Terrorism—The Hague 7 (4). org/https://doi.org/10.19165/2016.1.04.

Schoenholtz, Andrew. 2005. Refugee Protection in the United States Post-September 11. *Columbia Human Rights Law Review* 36: 323–364.

Schwartz, Felicia. 2017. State Department Dissent, Believed Largest Ever, Formally Lodged. *Wall Street Journal* February 1.

The Illegal Immigrant Reform and Immigrant Responsibility Act of 1996, Pub. L. No. 104–208, 110 Stat. 3009–546 (September 30, 1996). US Statutes at Large 110 (1996): 3009.

UNGA (UN General Assembly). 2013. Declaration of the High-level Dialogue on International Migration and Development. UN Doc. A/68/L.5. New York: UNGA.

UNHCR. 2019. Figures at a Glance. Available at: https://www.unhcr.org/figures-at-a-glance.html.

UNHCR. 2019a. Refugee Resettlement Facts. Available at:https://www.unhcr.org/resettlement-in-the-united-states.html.

USCIRF. 2005. Study on Asylum Seekers in Expedited Removal As Authorized by Section 605 of the International Religious Freedom Act of 1998: Evaluation of Credible Fear Referral in Expedited Removal at Ports of Entry in the United States, Report, Washington, D.C.

White House. 2015. National Security Strategy. Washington, DC: White House. Available at: https://obamawhitehouse.archives.gov/sites/default/files/docs/2015_national_security_strategy_2.pdf.

Zieck, Marjoleine. 2013. The 1956 Hungarian Refugee Emergency, an Early and Instructive Case of Resettlement. *Amsterdam Law Forum* 5 (2): 45–63.

CHAPTER 5

Fortress Europe

On a crisp fall morning in 2016 at the Keleti Railway Station, Péter, my research assistant, and I were buying train tickets to visit a refugee camp in Bicske, a small town outside Budapest, when we spotted a poster aimed at recruiting 'border-hunters.' Next to it, behind a small table covered with pamphlets and brochures, sat a couple of recruiters. Intrigued by the huge poster and the stack of brochures, I nudged Péter to talk to the recruiters to learn more about this scheme.

We learned that the Hungarian police were recruiting 3,000 'border-hunters' to join some 10,000 police and soldiers patrolling a razor-wire fence built along the 175-meter long border with Serbia to stop refugees from crossing into Hungary. We were told that the 'border-hunters' must be high school graduates and would receive a six-month training to prepare them for the job. They will be earning approximately 200,000 HUF (EUR 620) a month. This is a little less than the average monthly salary of 292,000 HUF (EUR 933) (Woods 2017), but well above the minimum of 161,000 HUF guaranteed by Hungary for those with secondary education. There are also other perks: housing and clothing allowance, and discount on travel and cell phones. The recruiter could not—or did not want to—tell us how many people he managed to recruit.

In the summer of 2015, the same Keleti Railway Station the recruiters were operating from, became a *de facto* refugee camp for tens of thousands of people fleeing violence in the Middle East and Afghanistan.

E. M. Goździak, *Human Trafficking as a New (In)Security Threat*,
https://doi.org/10.1007/978-3-030-62873-4_5

However, by early 2017, the Hungarian border patrol reported detaining fewer than 200 refugees reaching Hungary's southern border with Serbia a day. Ten thousand police and three thousand 'border-hunters' to deal with a couple hundred refugees. Many Hungarians point out that there are so few refugees trying to get into Hungary precisely because the border is so tightly guarded.

Having been born and lived in communist Poland for several decades, I am amazed that a country that once sat behind the Iron Curtain has adopted a 'build-a-wall' mentality to keep out refugees and asylum seekers. My Hungarian friends remind me that Viktor Orbán, the Prime Minister of Hungary, has been building Fortress Hungary for some time now. Hungarian border police, guns in holsters, swagger in pairs alongside the fence in a scene reminiscent of the Cold War. The 'border-hunters' are equipped with night-vision goggles, body heat detectors, and migrant-sniffing dogs.

At a swearing-in ceremony of border hunters in Budapest in the spring of 2017, a few months after our encounter with the recruiters, Viktor Orbán, whose anti-immigrant policies have gone down well with voters, said Hungary had to act to defend itself. The storm has not died, it has only subsided temporarily, he said. There are still millions waiting to set out on their journey in the hope of a better life (in Europe) (Than 2017).

Closing borders and building fences are not the only strategies to keep refugees at bay. Conceptualizing refugees and asylum seekers as victims of human trafficking and the smugglers that assist them in reaching Europe as traffickers is another tactic deployed by politicians and policy-makers. The narratives go further and posit that among the trafficked victims are terrorists. While 90% of irregular migrants use smugglers at some point in their journeys, terrorist groups are highly unlikely to use smuggling routes to infiltrate Europe, as terrorists often hold European citizenship or long-term residence permits (Garavoglia 2016).

In this chapter, I look at two European countries—Hungary and Poland—to showcase how human trafficking has replaced or been conflated with migration in the public narratives, policy responses, and practice with refugees. I chose Hungary and Poland, two countries with virtually no refugees and immigrants, to illustrate the baseless fear of the Other that allegedly poses a threat to European values, social cohesion, and national security.

Policing and Fortifying Borders

Border controls have been irrevocably linked to contemporary security discourses (Salvatori and Sanchez-Incera 2018). The link between migration and criminal activities, originally present mainly in the rhetoric of right-wing fringe parties, has found its way into the political mainstream on both sides of the Atlantic Ocean. When Viktor Orbán, Jarosław Kaczyński, or Donald Trump talk about migrants, they inevitably imply that migrants are criminals: terrorists, rapists, and thieves. Thus, borders need to be fortified to keep them at bay.

By the end of 2015, over 390,000 mainly Muslim refugees and asylum seekers crossed the Serbian-Hungarian border and descended on the Keleti Railway Station in Budapest. Only a fraction of the arrivals received permanent residency status (KSH.hu, n.d.). Yet, for Viktor Orbán, the arrival of refugees was not a humanitarian challenge but a Muslim invasion that required an appropriate response: closing the Balkan land route to the European Union.

Yet, somehow, this was not 'enough' as evidenced by the desire to recruit 3,000 'border-hunters' to join the 10,000 police and soldiers already patrolling the border (Goździak 2017), parts of which have recently been electrified. These actions stand in sharp contrast with the events of 1989, when Hungary opened its border with Austria and let thousands of East Germans through to West Germany (Haraszti 2015). While it is true that the unprecedented influx of refugees and asylum seekers in 2015 did result in at least a handful of jihadi terrorists entering the Schengen Zone through Hungary,[1] the government has systematically used the arrival of refugees as an opportunity to strengthen their Christian discourse—linking Christianity with the nation (kereszteny-nemzeti eszme) (Fekete 2016: 40)—and simultaneously stigmatizing refugees as terrorists. The conservative media likened the recent migration with the Ottoman era "when Hungary was a 'bastion,' defending Christianity from 'Muslim hordes'" (Pall and Sayfo 2016: 6). Antal Rogán, at the time leader of the Hungarian Fidesz' parliamentary group, warned of a future 'United European Caliphate' (Villányi 2015), while former Secretary of State László L. Simon urged Hungarians to make more babies in

[1] At least 14 jihadi terrorists responsible for the 2015 Paris and Brussels attacks entered Schengen through Hungary and spent several weeks in Budapest before continuing on to Belgium (lemonde.fr 2016).

order to counter the negative cultural effects of mass migration such as the envisioned 'impending victory of Islamic parties imposing polygamy and destroying the remainder of European culture' (Simon 2015: 231). The political rhetoric included both national security concerns and cultural insecurity. Beyond political statements, armed military police patrols on the streets of Budapest, in metro stations and in public spaces, have become a regular sight, as is the case in Paris and Brussels, while Hungary has yet to experience a terrorist attack.

The emphasis on policing borders and introducing military measures is based on the idea that criminals and terrorists can be found among refugees seeking safe haven in Europe. But as Patrick Kingsley, a journalist writing about migration for the *Guardian*, points out, building a fence along the Hungarian border will only shift refugees west to Croatia and Slovenia (Kingsley 2017: 225).

I got a glimpse at the ways Viktor Orbán manipulated the discourse about refugees in 2016 while in Budapest as the George Soros Visiting Chair in Public Policy. A couple of weeks after my arrival, Orbán called for a national referendum and asked Hungarians a simple question: "Do you want the European Union to prescribe the mandatory settlement of non-Hungarian citizens in Hungary without the consent of the National Assembly?".

Voter turnout was poor. A mere 39% Hungarians voted, far short of the 50% participation required to make the referendum valid under Hungarian law. Never one to let facts get in the way of politics, Orbán, whose Eurosceptic Fidesz party has more support than all opposition parties combined, said in a televised speech:

> The European Union's proposal is to let the migrants in and distribute them in mandatory fashion among the member states and for Brussels to decide about this distribution. Hungarians today considered this proposal and they rejected it. Hungarians decided that only we, Hungarians, can decide with whom we want to live. The question was 'Brussels or Budapest' and we decided this issue is exclusively the competence of Budapest.

Orbán decided that the 3.3 million Hungarians who voted "No" in the referendum spoke for the whole country of 10 million Hungarians. After his speech, there were fireworks over the Danube river in the colors of the Hungarian flag.

The Hungarian anti-immigrant campaign started in early 2015, shortly after the terrorist attack in Paris on the offices of *Charlie Hebdo*. In a TV interview, Viktor Orbán said that "[I] would like to keep Hungary as the country of Hungarians" (Bocskor 2018: 557), indicating that there is no room in Hungary for any ethnic or religious minorities. This speech framed immigration as a security issue, emphasizing that immigration and terrorism go hand-in-hand, that immigrants adversely affect the labor market, and increase crime rates (Sik et al. 2016 cited in Bocskor 2018).

Between April 24 and July 27, 2015, the government conducted a national consultation on immigration and terrorism. A survey was mailed to all Hungarians 18 years of age and above to answer 12 multiple-choice questions such as: Do you agree that ill-conceived immigration policies contribute to the spread of terrorism? Do you think that keeping illegal immigrants in custody round-the-clock should be made possible? The letter that accompanied the survey referred to refugees as economic migrants trying to cross the border illegally and gain access to social benefits in Europe. The letter also intimated that refugees and asylum seekers harbor terrorists, that they pose a "threat" and "must be stopped" (Bocskor 2018: 560–561).

As the survey was being mailed to all adult Hungarians, large billboards were being erected all over the country warning immigrants—in Hungarian [sic!]—not to steal jobs from Hungarians and to respect Hungarian law and culture. The Two-Tailed Dog Party (Magyar Kétfarkú Kutya Párt), a joke political party, erected their own billboards with messages such as "If you are the prime minister of Hungary you have to protect our laws" and "Immigrants do not take our jobs." The United Nations High Commissioner for Refugees (UNHCR) joined the billboard campaign with their own posters. The national campaign cost 960 million HUF. Only one million of the eight million recipients filled out and mailed the questionnaire back (Kiss 2016). Nevertheless, Viktor Orbán continued to build Fortress Hungary.

Closing Refugee Camps

Erecting fences, rejecting asylum applications to keep refugees out is one strategy, closing down existing refugee camps is another. In addition to recruiting border hunters and building fences, Victor Orbán has closed most refugee camps. The camp in Bicske Péter and I visited, operated as a refugee facility for over two decades. In the little museum established by refugees on the premises of the reception center one was able to see artifacts, coins, and paintings from many parts of the world: several countries in Africa, the Middle East, Bosnia, Kosovo, and Afghanistan, to name a few examples. However, in December 2016, the camp was shut down as part of a government-mandated wave of camp closures. When I visited the camp a few days before it closed, 75 individuals, hailing from Cuba, Nigeria, Cameroon, Iraq, Pakistan, and Afghanistan, lived there.

At the time of my visit, Bicske, which could house as many as 460 refugees, was operating well below capacity. The number of asylum applicants in the country has decreased dramatically. According to data from the Hungarian Helsinki Committee, in October 2016, 1,198 refugees registered for asylum in Hungary compared with 5,812 in April 2016. As of October 2016, there were 529 asylum seekers staying in Hungarian refugee reception facilities: 318 at open reception centers such as Bicske and 211 in detention centers (personal communication 2016).

The refugees I chatted with, a couple from Nigeria and a young family from Cuba, among others, were no terrorists. Jose's elderly mother had received permission to stay in Budapest a couple of years before and Jose, his wife, and their toddler daughter were hopeful that they would be able to reunite with her. Jose is a computer programmer and is confident that he will have no problem finding a job. In addition to his native Spanish, he speaks English and is now also learning Hungarian. Jose doesn't pose a threat to anyone. He is fleeing persecution in Cuba. The Nigerian couple fled northern Nigeria when Boko Haram killed several members of their family. They mean no harm to anybody; all they want is to live in peace.

When the camp in Bicske closed, the refugees were relocated to a camp in Kiskunhalas in southern Hungary, some two and a half hours by train from Budapest. Not an optimal location. The Bicske camp's location offered its residents opportunities to access a variety of educational and recreational activities that helped them adjust to life in Hungary. Some refugees commuted to Budapest to attend classes at the Central European University (CEU) as well as language courses provided by nongovernmental organizations (NGOs). Bicske residents often attended events and met with Hungarian mentors from groups such as Artemisszió, a multicultural foundation, and MigSzol, a migrant advocacy group. Christian refugees were bused to an American church each Sunday morning. Moving the residents to Kiskunhalas deprived them of these opportunities. The Hungarian government offers very few resources to asylum seekers, both to those in reception facilities awaiting decisions on their cases and those who have received asylum in Hungary. Access to the civil society organizations helping refugees prepare for their new lives is key.

Criminalizing Assistance to Refugees

While help from civil society organizations and Good Samaritans is crucial for refugees and asylum seekers in Hungary, recent legislation has seriously curtailed the ability of civil society to provide assistance to undocumented migrants. In June of 2018, the Hungarian Parliament approved a package of laws called the "Stop Soros" bill that criminalizes assistance to undocumented migrants and creates a parallel court system to try those who attempt to provide assistance to migrants. Many fear that this new legislation "will be used for politically sensitive cases, accelerating efforts by Prime Minister Viktor Orbán to transform the country into what he calls an 'illiberal democracy'" (Kingsley 2018).

Ironically, the new legislation passed on World Refugee Day. "It is a bitter irony that as the world marks World Refugee Day, the Hungarian Parliament voted today to introduce a law that targets organizations and individuals who support asylum-seekers, refugees and migrants," said Amnesty International's Europe director, Gauri van Gulik (cited in Than 2018). Under the new law, assisting migrants to legalize their status in Hungary by, for example, distributing information about the asylum process or providing them with financial assistance, could result in a 12-months jail term.

The "Stop Soros" legislation has been condemned by the United Nations, which also criticized Mr. Orbán for his efforts to crack down on the homeless within the same legislative package, and Amnesty International as well as other human rights organizations. Patrick Gaspard, president of the Open Society Foundations, said: "Migration is clearly being used by the Hungarian government as a political diversion. The ultimate objective is to intimidate civil society and muzzle independent critics, including those who receive some of their funding from Open Society. We will continue to fund their important work at this difficult time, and do what we can to support Hungary's courageous rights defenders" (cited in Than 2018).

Viktor Orbán's government has also amended the constitution to state that an "alien population" cannot be settled in Hungary, rejecting European Union quotas to settled refugees in the region. The government said the bill intends to deter illegal immigration, which threatens Hungary's security, erodes European stability, and risks undermining Hungary's Christian values.

No to Refugees, Yes to Migrants with Money

While Mr. Orbán vehemently opposes finding homes for 1,294 refugees that the EU asked Hungary to assist, he welcomes foreigners who are able to buy the right to live in Hungary. Since 2012, Viktor Orbán's government has been selling government bonds worth about €300,000 ($331,000) that essentially act as resident permits for foreign investors. Apparently, some 10,000 Chinese have taken advantage of the scheme to move to Hungary as did smaller numbers of affluent investors from Russia and the Middle East. Imre Hamar, Director of the Confucius Institute in Budapest, said the following about the Chinese migrants:

> Those who come to Hungary like this are quite different from the first wave of migration 25 years ago - they are very, very rich. They don't just buy one apartment, but two or three in the best districts of Budapest. I know of one who has opened a tea house. He has a big tea house chain in China where he made a fortune and he's opened a small shop here - more for fun than for money.

The Chinese investors are considered a threat neither to national security nor to cultural cohesion, unlike refugees and migrants from the Middle East.

Ironically, in the second part of the twentieth century, Hungary built strong political and economic relationships with several Middle Eastern countries. Many students from Arab countries—Algeria, Syria, and Iraq—studied at universities in Budapest, Debrecen, and Pécs, pursuing engineering and medical degrees. Some of them married Hungarians and settled in the country (Pall and Sayfo 2016). By the mid-2010s, Jobbik, the far-right political party, forged strong ties with Muslim countries, inviting Iranian President Mahmoud Ah-madinejad to send observers to monitor the 2009 European parliamentary elections (Political Radical 2014). The party's sympathy with Islam isolated Jobbik from the mainstream European far-right. Today, the Hungarian government continues its efforts to strengthen economic ties with Muslim countries in the Middle East and Asia–Azerbaijan, Kazakhstan, Turkey, Turkmenistan, and Saudi Arabia (Éltető and Völgyi 2013) and highlights the importance of a dialogue between different cultures (Daily News Hungary 2016) in the international arena. The Orbán government has been promoting a policy of 'Eastern-opening' in order to secure new export markets for Hungarian products. However, Mr. Orbán and his government do not want to see any Middle Eastern refugees or immigrants on the Hungarian soil.

Viktor Orbán is promoting his strategies—militarization of borders, closure of refugee camps, strict immigration policies—among leaders of the other Visegrád Four countries: Poland, the Czech Republic, and Slovakia. Anti-immigrant sentiments and xenophobic rhetoric are on the rise in Poland where Mr. Orbán's friend, Jarosław Kaczyński, the Chairman of the ruling Law and Justice party, spews the same hatred of Muslim refugees.

While the EU institutions, including the European Commission and Council, have remained virtually silent on the hate campaigns spreading in Central Europe, they have spoken on the issue of walls and fences. In his 2015 State of Union speech before the European Parliament, European Commission President Juncker stated that "walls and fences have no place in EU Member States" (Carrera et al. 2015).

A Road to Nowhere: Asylum Seekers at the Brześć-Terespol Border Crossing

Unlike Hungary, Poland has not built a fence along its borders. However, in 2017 more than a million Polish Catholics, representing 320 churches from 22 dioceses, held rosary prayers in roughly 4,000 locations along the country's 2,000-mile border with Germany, the Czech Republic, Slovakia, Ukraine, Belarus, Lithuania, Russia, and the Baltic Sea to implore the Virgin Mary to protect the country from the invasion by Muslim refugees (see Bourne 2017).

And then there is the border crossing from Belarus to Poland in Brześć-Terespol (Ciobanu 2017; Lipczak 2018). This particular border crossing has been a main entry point for Chechens, Tajiks, and others from the post-Soviet region for many years. In 2016 alone, some 85,000 asylum seekers attempted to enter Poland in the hopes to reach the EU territory. Recently, however, the Polish border guards have been pushing the majority of asylum seekers back, allowing, on average, two refugee families per day to enter Poland. The pushbacks constitute de facto *refoulement*, despite the fact that the principle of *non-refoulement*[2] is the cornerstone of refugee protection enshrined in the 1951 Refugee Convention and the 1967 Protocol, both of which Poland acceded to in 1991. According to the 2017 Human Rights Watch report, between August and September 2016, as many as 3,000 asylum seekers and migrants were turned back at the border crossing and stranded in the Belarusian border town Brest/Brześć. In the same year, Poland's recognition rate for asylum seekers from Russia (including Chechens) was 5.6% and for those from Tajikistan, 10.5%. This compares with an average across the EU 28 member states of 19% for asylum seekers from Russia and 27.5%3 for those from Tajikistan (HRW 2017). The pushbacks and the high rates of asylum application rejections met with little protest from European leaders who have their own interests in keeping the bloc's eastern border shut (Ciobanu 2017).

On the few occasions when European institutions reacted to the situation on the Polish-Belarussian border, the Polish authorities ignored their decision. When the case of "Hamid K," a Chechen asylum seeker, who tried to enter Poland 31 times, ended up in the European Court for Human Rights, the court prohibited Polish authorities to return him to Belarus. However, the Polish government ignored the order saying that the war in Chechnya ended in 2009, so Chechens—who are officially Russian citizens—are no longer asylum seekers, but labor migrants (Lipczak 2018).

While some would like to portray Chechens as Muslim terrorists who should not be allowed to enter Europe, others conceptualize them as separatists attempting to achieve freedom from Russia (Shinar 2019), and still others point out the dangers that await Chechen asylum seekers back in Chechnya.

Iwona Kaliszewska, an anthropologist at the Warsaw University, and Maciej Falkowski, currently a diplomat in Erevan, have reported extensively on the situation in Chechnya (Kaliszewska and Falkowski 2010). Kaliszewska asserts that ruled by Kremlin-backed Kadyrov, Chechnya is a place of human rights violations, political persecution, torture and forced disappearances. The country is also unsafe for domestic violence victims

[2] Non-refoulement is a fundamental principle of international law that forbids a country receiving asylum seekers from returning them to a country where they would be in danger of persecution based on race, religion, nationality, membership of a particular social group or political opinion.

where violence against women goes unpunished. There are people fleeing honor crimes and unsettled personal feuds, dating back to the war, that are often solved using the state apparatus of violence, says Kaliszewska. And finally, there are the Salafis, the followers of a purist movement within Sunni Islam, considered terrorists by Kadyrov, who promotes 'traditional Chechen Islam,' inspired by practices of the mystical Sufi order, Qadiriya. Arrests or extrajudicial killings of Salafis boost the statistics of the 'war on terror.' Chechnya's 'anti-terrorist actions' are handsomely rewarded by Kremlin (Kaliszewska 2017).

Contrary to the evidence provided by researchers on the ground, the then Polish Minister of Internal Affairs, Mariusz Błaszczak, stated in a media interview on August 2016 that Poland would not accept refugees from Chechnya, because they were a threat to national security (HRW 2017). It seems that the Polish authorities cannot decide whether the Chechens are labor migrants or national security threats. Whatever the label, activists emphasize that authorities abuse the human rights of individuals and families presenting at the Belorussian-Polish border in order to cross to Poland to launch their asylum claim.

The situation at the Brześć-Terespol crossing has been worsening since 2015. This border crossing is endemic of the security that has become a new super value overriding others, such as respect for human dignity, freedom, equality, the rule of law, and respect for human rights. Some asylum seekers have been pushed back from the border 80 times, despite the fact that according to national and international law, foreigners should be allowed to enter the territory of Poland, where the competent administrative authority, in this case the Office for Foreigners, could verify presented information and decide whether asylum seekers will be granted refugee status or subsidiary protection. Marta Górczyńska, a lawyer at the Helsinki Foundation for Human Rights (HFHR), said: "The conduct of Border Guard officers from the branch in Terespol, violates both the provisions of national law, as well as EU and international law." "The actions of the Polish Border Guards are part of a wider, unruly practice that is now also used by other countries of our region, consisting of pushing back foreigners seeking protection in the European Union," she added. Her colleague at the HFHR, Marta Sczepaniak, and co-author of the report "A Road to Nowhere" (Górczyńska and Szczepanik 2016), added: "The majority of the asylum seekers are large families from Chechnya. Their situation is getting worse from day to day. Some have spent all their money waiting for months in Belarus. They are now forced to live at the railway. There are many children in this group."

Frustrated by the situation at the border, in 2016, 200 Chechens erected a camp on the Belarusian side of the border and demanded refugee status. Ramzan Kadyrow, the President of Chechnya, commented that calling the Chechens refugees is "inappropriate," because they are being protected and provided for at home. Abdullah, interviewed by TVN24.pl, said: "today, you are talking to your friend, but tomorrow he may just mysteriously disappear." The official reason Abdullah was pushed back from the border was "lack of visa." "How can a refugee get a visa?" asks Abdullah. "Chechens cannot obtain a visa to go to Poland."

Islamophobia Without Muslims

With Chechens stuck at the border and very few refugees from the Middle East coming to Poland, the migration that is occurring elsewhere in Europe has been greatly politicized, especially by the populist national-conservative Law and Justice party, KORWiN, and far-right groups that formed part of Kukiz'15. Political candidates expressed openly xenophobic, racist, and Islamophobic views, produced anti-immigration posters, and participated in demonstrations "against the Islamization of Poland and Europe" (Pędziwiatr 2015). Kamil Kupiec, representing the KORWiN party in Kraków, used an electoral poster that read "Instead of immigrants we want repatriates." Ewa Damaszek, also from KORWiN, proclaimed "Silesia is our home. Islam has its own." Ms. Damaszek is referring here to people of Polish origin whose ancestors have relocated to Kazakhstan, Siberia, Azerbaijan, or other countries.

The European Union asked Poland to accept 6,500 refugees. The proposed quota constitutes less than 0.02% of the Polish population of 40 million, but has sparked a lot of outrage. The anti-refugee rally in November 2015 in the city of Wrocław captured the populism that has been on display in Poland in the last couple of years. Thousands of protesters marched, denouncing the EU proposal. The rally members chanted anti-Islam and anti-migrant slogans declaring their loyalty to 'God, Honor, and Fatherland.' They finished the gathering by burning an effigy—not of a Muslim or a refugee, but a Hassidic Jew—wrapped in the EU flag (Tharoor 2016).

In a YouTube chat, Jarosław Kaczyński, the chairman of the Law and Justice party, said: "After recent events connected with acts of terror,

[Poland] will not accept refugees because there is no mechanism that would ensure security" (Kaczyński 2016). Kaczyński also rejected the EU suggestion that countries which do not want to accept refugees should pay a certain amount of money for each asylum seeker they turn away. According to Eurostat (2015), Poland accepted just 0.21 asylum seekers per 1,000 citizens, compared to 0.5 per thousand in the United Kingdom or 8.43 in Sweden. Many Poles agree with the party leadership. More than half of Poles surveyed by the Center for Public Opinion Research (CBOS) in 2017 were adamant that Poland should not admit any refugees; 40% of the respondents agreed the country should provide temporary refuge until it is safe for the refugees to go back home. Only 4% of the survey participants favored permanent resettlement of refugees in Poland. A higher proportion of respondents—almost two-thirds—were against relocating to Poland Middle Eastern and Northern African refugees already in the European Union. Only 28% of the survey respondents thought that Poland should share the responsibility with other EU countries and accept some of the refugees (CBOS 2017). Debates observed in the public sphere—on Polish TV, in churches, and cafes—centered on rejecting Muslim refugees and allowing Christians from the Middle East to settle in Poland. The Warsaw-based Estera Foundation proclaimed that they would support resettlement of Christians from Syria. Miriam Shaded, the head of Estera, said that Muslim refugees pose a threat to Poland: "They [non-Christian refugees] can be a threat to Poland. I think it is a great way for ISIS to locate their troops… all around Europe" (Wasik and Foy 2015).

A study financed by the Visegrád Fund and conducted between July 2016 and June 2017, examined opinions of young people (17- to 30-year old) about the recent 'migration crisis.' In Poland, young people were almost equally divided between those who would accept refugees from countries affected by armed conflict (43%) and those who would not (46%). When asked if they were ready to welcome refugees into their neighborhoods, 43% indicated they were not ready, while 41% said they would receive refugees; 16% said they did not know what they would do (Visegrád Fund 2017). Unfortunately, the study did not provide information on educational levels of the youth who participated in the survey. It would be interesting to know whether education affected people's opinions. While the vast majority (75%) of the Polish youth did not notice more refugees in their local area, 66.7% affirmed that there are no positive effects stemming from arrival of refugees. The researchers involved in the study attributed these statements to the power of media discourses that portray refugees in very negative light. In my own research, I have also seen negative effects of media, especially social media, on attitudes toward refugees. According to the Visegrád study, young Poles are mainly afraid of cultural and religious tensions (82.5%), followed by increase in crime (65.1%), and terrorist attacks (58.7%).

Poles also see Muslim men as a threat to the safety of Polish women. In the winter of 2016, shortly after the alleged mass sexual assaults of women in Cologne on the 2015 New Year's Eve, a popular right-wing Polish weekly, wSieci (The Network) published a deeply provocative magazine cover. It showed a young blonde woman, garbed loosely in the EU flag, being groped by three men. The cover line read: "The Islamic Rape of Europe." The magazine echoed the sentiments of Polish right-wing groups, both secular and Catholic, who portrayed Muslim men as polygamous and abusive, and an imminent threat to the safety of Polish (and more generally, white European) women. While the magazine cover might be connected with the sexual assaults in Germany, the magazine's rendition of a young white woman, violated by dark-skinned men, is also eerily reminiscent of the nationalist propaganda of the World War II era with its imagery of a scheming Jewish spider eyeing a blonde Fräulein or a French colonial soldier groping a fair-skinned girl (Taroon 2016).

The call to protect Polish women from 'wild Muslim men' is happening at the same time when women's rights in Poland are being severely curtailed. In October 2017, police in several Polish cities raided offices of the Women's Rights Centre and Baba, two nongovernmental organizations that support domestic violence victims and promote women's rights (Bielecka 2017). While some called the reports fake news (Młynarz 2017), Polish parliamentarians periodically do call for Poland's withdrawal from the Istanbul Convention (EU News 2016), a treaty aimed at preventing violence against women, supporting survivors, and holding perpetrators to account. The Polish Catholic Church claims the Convention is a source of evil 'gender ideology' aimed at destroying Polish traditional values (Komosa 2014).

Traffickers or Smugglers? Friends of Foes?

The narratives about human trafficking not only criminalize or victimize refugees and migrants, but they also often conflate smugglers with traffickers. Don't get me wrong, the conditions under which refugees and migrants travel to Europe are difficult and dangerous. But are the people who facilitate these journeys traffickers? Do they pass muster of the trafficking definition? Do they force, defraud, and coerce refugees and migrants to embark on the perilous journeys?

Interviews with refugees who made it to Europe and journalistic accounts suggest that "the people we call 'human traffickers' are usually not much more than informal networks of expensive 'travel agents'" (Dalakoglou and Alexandridis 2015). A young Syrian man who made it to Istanbul told me that without his smuggler he would have perished in Aleppo. On the other hand, the same young man felt deceived by the smuggler who told him the journey would be very short, while in fact it took much longer (personal communication 2017).

Dalakoglou and Alexandridis (2015) argue that the "horrendous conditions under which this mobility takes place are a by-product of the effort to evade national and international border policing and visa policies." In other words, the militarization of borders creates business for these 'human traffickers.' Having elevated the refugee flight from wars to human trafficking, the EU responded to this 'crisis' by bolstering its marine border patrols in the Mediterranean, strengthening FRONTEX, the European Border and Coast Guard Agency, erecting razor-wire-topped fences rather than trying to respect the human rights of the refugees seeking safety in Europe. These strategies have resulted in a decreased number of refugees reaching European shores, but the rate of fatalities *en route* has gone up dramatically, according to the UNHCR report *Desperate Journeys* (UNHCR 2018).

Crimmigration

The situation in Hungary and Poland is emblematic of what Juliet Stumpf (2006) called "crimmigration" or the merger of crime control and immigration law. In this conceptualization, migrants have become increasingly subject to criminalization for what once were considered administrative immigration infractions. Scholars studying crimmigration emphasize that the approach is that more and more criminal law measures are applied to persons who have not committed crimes unrelated to their desire to seek safe haven or better livelihoods in a country of their choice and are punished solely because they circumvented immigration rules and border controls (Barker 2017; Nagy 2016; Klaus 2017).

What is fascinating about Hungary and Poland, two post-socialist states in Central Europe, is how the politics of penal reform, rather than rejecting the repressive past and advocating for milder punishments, instead embraced a more punitive response to transitional and social insecurities. By tracing political discourses around crime and anxieties around migration, Lynne Haney (2016) shows how punishment became a preferred tool to settle political crises and threats of Europeanization. Politicians were able to "equate punitiveness with national sovereignty and protection" (Haney 2016: 346). Haney calls this process "penal nationalism" to show how penal power is used to help redefine Central European states and social relations outside a socialist or EU frame.

Links between crime, security, migration, and integration are far from new (Tonry 1997). They were first established in the context of the 'asylum crisis' of the 1990s and have escalated since the beginning of the current 'refugee crises' in Europe. The examples discussed in this chapter show how the assumption that foreigners may indeed be criminals or may have committed entry-related crimes, including people smuggling and trafficking (see Nagy 2016) contributed to the conceptualization of various forms of migration as a security issue. The new crimmigration policies have also fed the xenophobic public discourses in Central Europe and beyond.

References

Barker, Vanessa. 2017. Penal Power at the Border: Realigning State and Nation. *Theoretical Criminology* 21 (4): 441–457.

Bielecka A. 2017. Poland No Friend to Women. Government Refuses to Fund Women's Support Groups. Human Rights Watch, December 3. Available at: https://www.hrw.org/news/2017/12/03/poland-no-friend-women. Accessed March 2, 2018.

Bocskor, Akos. 2018. Anti-Immigrant Discourses in Hungary During the "Crisis" Year: The Orbán Government's 'National Consultation' Campaign of 2015. *Sociology* 52 (3): 551–568.

Bourne, Lisa. 2017. Massive Turnout for Rosary Crusade in Poland. Liberals Furious. *Life Site News*, October 9. Available at: https://www.lifesitenews.com/news/massive-turnout-for-rosary-crusade-in-poland.-liberals-furious.

Carrera, Sergio, Steven Blockmans, Daniel Gros, and Elspeth Guild. 2015. The EU's Response to the Refugee Crisis Taking Stock and Setting Policy Priorities. CEPS Essay No. 20, December 16.

CBOS. 2017. *Stosunek Polaków do przyjmowania uchodźców*. Warsaw: Fundacja Centrum Badania Opinii Społecznej.

Ciobanu, Claudia. 2017. Poland Seals Europe's Eastern Frontier as E.U. Turns a Blind Eye. *Refugees Deeply*, April 26. Available at: https://www.newsdeeply.com/refugees/articles/2017/04/26/poland-seals-europes-eastern-frontier-as-e-u-turns-a-blind-eye.

Daily News Hungary. 2016. Orbán Holds Talks with Religious Leaders. *Daily News Hungary*, June 2. Available at: https://bit.ly/2bDCB4p. Accessed on May 26, 2017.

Dalakoglou, Dimitris and Alexandridis, Antonios. 2015. Fortress Europe Continues to Treat Migrants as Criminals. *The Conversation*. https://theconversation.com/fortress-europe-continues-to-treat-migrants-as-criminals-49026.

Éltető, A., and K. Völgyi. 2013. 'Keleti Nyitás' a Számok Tükrében-Külkereskedelem Ázsiával. *Külgazdaság* 57 (7–8): 67–104.

Eurostat. 2015. Asylum in the EU. Available at: https://ec.europa.eu/eurostat/documents/2995521/6751779/3-20032015-BP-EN.pdf/35e04263-2db5-4e75-b3d3-6b086b23ef2b. Accessed on 15 May 2017.

Fekete, L. 2016. Hungary: Power, Punishment, and the 'Christian-National Idea.' *Race & Class* 57 (4): 39–53.

Garavoglia, Matteo. 2016. Securing Europe's Borders. The First Step to a Comprehensive Asylum Policy. *Foreign Affairs*, April 29. Available at: https://www.foreignaffairs.com/articles/europe/2016-04-29/securing-europes-borders.

Górczyńska, Marta, and Marta Szczepanik. 2016. A Road to Nowhere. The Account of a Monitoring Visit at the Brześć-Terespol Border Crossing Between Poland and Belarus. Helsinki Foundation for Human Rights. Available at: https://www.hfhr.pl/wp-content/uploads/2016/11/raport-droga-donikad-EN-web.pdf.

Goździak, E. 2017. Let's Make Europe Great Again! *Anthropology News*, March 6. Available at: https://www.anthropology-news.org/index.php/2017/03/06/lets-make-europe-great-again/. Accessed on June 15, 2017.

Haney, Lynne. 2016. Prisons of the Past: Penal Nationalism and the Politics of Punishment in Central Europe. *Punishment & Society* 18 (3): 346–368.

Haraszti, M. 2015. Behind Viktor Orbán's War on Refugees in Hungary. Available at: https://www.huffingtonpost.com/miklos-haraszti/viktor-orban-hungary-refugees_b_8100906.html. Accessed on September 14, 2017.

Human Rights Watch (HRW). 2017. Poland: Asylum Seekers Blocked at Border. Available at: https://www.hrw.org/news/2017/03/01/poland-asylum-seekers-blocked-border.

Kaczyński J. 2016. Silna Polska w Europie. Czat z Jarosławem Kaczyńskim. Online: https://www.youtube.com/watch?v=RlwmaTLlLj4. Accessed on June 15, 2017.

Kaliszewska, Iwona. 2017. Przed czym uciekają Czeczeni koczujący na dworcu w Brześciu? Opowiada Iwona Kaliszewska w rozmowie z Karoliną Głowacką. Podcast available at: https://audycje.tokfm.pl/podcast/Przed-czym-uciekaja-Czeczeni-koczujacy-na-dworcu-w-Brzesciu-Opowiada-Iwona-Kaliszewska-w-rozmowie-z-Karolina-Glowacka/48541

Kaliszewska, Iwona, and Maciej Falkowski. 2010. *Matrioszka w hidżabie. Zbiór reportaży z Dagestanu i Czeczenii*. Warszawa: Wydawnictwo Sic!

Kingsley, Patrick. 2017. *The New Odyssey. The Story of the Twenty-First-Century Refugee Crisis*. Liveright Publishing Corporation: New York.

Kingsley, Patrick. 2018. Hungary Criminalizes Aiding Illegal Immigrants. *The New York Times*, June 20.

Kiss, Eszter. 2016. The Hungarians Have Decided: They Do Not Want Illegal Migrants: Media Representation of the Hungarian Governmental Anti-immigration Campaign. *Acta Humana* 4 (6): 45–77.

Klaus, Witold. 2017. Security First: New Right-Wing Government in Poland and Its Policy Towards Immigrants and Refugees. *Surveillance and Society* 15 (3/4): 523–528.

Komosa, A. 2014. Co ma gender do przemocy wobec kobiet? Konwencja o zwalczaniu przemocy ciągle dzieli. Availabe at: https://natemat.pl/117841,co-ma-gender-do-przemocy-wobec-kobiet-europejska-konwencja-o-zwalczaniu-i-zapobieganiu-przemocy-wobec-kobiet-wciaz-budzi-kontrow. Accessed on April 30, 2018.

Lipczak, Aleksandra. 2018. The Invisible Refugee Crisis on Poland's Doorstep. *UnHerd*, August 29. Available at: https://unherd.com/2018/08/invisible-refugee-crisis-polands-doorstep/.

Młynarz, W. 2017. Nowoczesna rozprzestrzenia 'fake news'? Kulisy manipulacji w sprawie 'zastraszania kobiecych organizacji. Available at: https://www.stefczyk.info/wiadomosci/polska/czy-nowoczesna-rozprzestrzenia-fake-news-kulisy-manipulacji,21339145062. Accessed on June 18, 2018.

Nagy, Boldizsár. 2016. Hungarian Asylum Law and Policy in 2015–2016: Securitization Instead of Loyal Cooperation. *German Law Journal* 17 (6): 1033–1081.

Pall, Z., and O. Sayfo. 2016. Why an Anti-Islam Campaign Has Taken Root in Hungary, a Country with Few Muslims. Available at: https://visegradrevue.eu/why-an-anti-islam-campaign-has-taken-root-in-hungary-a-coun-try-with-few-muslims/. Accessed on September 15, 2017.

Pędziwiatr, K. 2015. Islamophobia in Poland 2015 Report. In *European Islamophobia Report*, ed. E. Bayrakli and F. Hafez, 425–441. Istanbul: SETA.

Salvatori, Maria Vitorria, and Letitia Sanchez Incera. 2018. Beyond Fortress Europe. The Theory and Policy of Border Control. Available at: https://www.eurozine.com/beyond-fortress-europe/

Shinar, Chaim. 2019. Chechens: Freedom Fighters or Terrorists? *European Review* 27 (1): 131–142.

Sik, Endre, B. Simonovits, and B. Szeitl. 2016. Az idegenellenesség alakulása és a bevándorlással kapcsolatos félelmek Magyarországon és a visegrádi országokban. *REGIO* 24 (2): 81–108.

Simon, L. 2015. Szaporodjunk! *Népszabadság Online*, September 5. Available at: https://nol.hu/video/lsimon-a-szaporodasban-latja-a-jovotl573295?utm_source=mandiner&utm_medium=link&utm_campaign=mandiner_201601. Accessed on May 5, 2017.

Stumpf, Juliet. 2006. The Crimmigration Crisis: Immigrants, Crime and Sovereign Power. Bepress Legal Series: Working Paper 1635. Berkeley, CA: Bepress Legal Repository. Available at: https://law.bepress.com/expresso/eps/1635.

Taroon, I. 2016. The So-Called 'Islamic Rape of Europe' Is Part of a Long and Racist History. *The Washington Post*, February 18. Available at: https://www.washingtonpost.com/news/worldviews/wp/2016/02/18/the-so-called-islamic-rape-of-europe-is-part-of-a-long-and-racist-history/?utm_term=.215a9b7ee349. Accessed on September 15, 2017.

Than, Krisztina. 2017. Hungary to Arm New 'Border Hunters' After Six-Month Crash Course. *World News*, March 9. Available at: https://www.reuters.com/article/us-europe-migrants-hungary-borderhunters-idUSKBN16G2ED.

Than, Krisztina. 2018. Hungary Aims to Criminalize Aiding Illegal Migration in 'Stop Soros' Bill. *World News*, May 29. Available at: https://www.reuters.com/article/us-hungary-soros-law/hungary-aims-to-criminalize-aiding-illegal-migration-in-stop-soros-bill-idUSKCN1IU1KE

Tharoor, I. 2016. The So-Called 'Islamic Rape of Europe' Is Part of a Long and Racist History. *The Washington Post*, February 18. Available at: https://www.washingtonpost.com/news/worldviews/wp/2016/02/18/the-so-called-islamic-rape-of-europe-is-part-of-a-long-and-racist-history/?utm_term=.853034263ae2. Accessed on May 26, 2017.

Tonry Michael. 1997. Ethnicity, Crime, and Immigration. *Crime Justice* 21: 1–29.

UNHCR. 2018. Desperate Journeys. Refugees and Migrants Arriving in Europe and at Europe's Borders. Available at: https://www.unhcr.org/desperatejourneys/.

Villányi K. 2015. Azt Akarjuk, Hogy Unokáink egy Európai Kalifátusban Éljenek? *Magyar Idők*, November 14. Available at: https://magyaridok.hu/belfold/azt-akarjuk-hogy-az-unokaink-egy-europai-kalifatusban-el-jenek-5035/. Accessed on June 15, 2017.

Visegrád Fund. 2017. Vision of Europe Through the Eyes of Young People from the States of the Visegrad Group. Available at: https://www.forumleaders.eu/projekty/v4/vision_of_the_europe_throught_the_eyes_of_young_people_from_the_states_of_the_visegrad_group.pdf. Accessed on September 14, 2017.

Wasik, Z., and H. Foy. 2015. Poland Favors Christian Refugees from Syria. *Financial Times*, August 21. Available at: https://www.ft.com/content/6edfdd30-472a-11e5-b3b2-1672f710807b. Accessed on June 15, 2017.

Woods, John. 2017. Average Salary 700 EUR in Hungary? *Daily News Hungary* November 26. Available at: https://dailynewshungary.com/hungarian-average-salary-700-eur/. Accessed on May 26, 2018.

PART III

Lived Experiences of (In)Security

Some scholars posit that security concerns over the past couple of decades have been shifting away from state-focused challenges, in which military forces have traditionally been the best form of protection, to human-centered security, in which instruments other than the military may prove the primary means of protection. In this part of the book, I focus on how (in)security is experienced by trafficked victims, irregular migrants, and asylum seekers in the United States and in Europe. This part of the book draws heavily on my empirical research with survivors of human trafficking and irregular migrants in the United States and in Europe. In Chapter 6, I discuss the violence and poverty in the Northern Triangle countries (Guatemala, Nicaragua, and El Salvador) and Mexico that prompted many young people, including underage youth, to seek safety and better livelihoods in the United States—only to be recruited by Mexican cartels and Central American gangs to cross people and drugs across the U.S. southern border. In Chapter 7, I look at the growing number of unaccompanied refugee and migrant children who have been arriving in Europe since 2015, discussing their lack of safety as they embark on perilous land and sea journeys destined for Europe and their continued insecurity on the European shores. I wonder why we depend so much on panic narratives that view 'traffickers' as the ultimate perpetrators of violence in the refugee crisis and a threat to the security of the European continent.

CHAPTER 6

Drug Mules, Foot Guides, or Victims of Child Trafficking?

Faced with rising numbers of migrants at the southern border, Donald Trump has repeatedly warned his supporters about an apocalyptic 'invasion' populated by criminals with face tattoos who look fearsome enough to be 'fighting for the UFC.' Trump's exaggerated statements have been contradicted many times, including by his own administration. In May 2019, Russell T. Vought, the acting director of the Office of Management and Budget (OMB), wrote in an emergency request for $4.5 billion to sustain critical and lifesaving missions at the border: "Immediate emergency action is required . . . to safely, securely, and humanely process and care for this at-risk migrant population" (Nakamura 2019).

While most of the asylum seekers at the border, as well as those who managed to cross the frontier in the past, pose no security threat to the country, on occasion, immigration officers find among Mexican and Central American unaccompanied adolescents drug mules or foot guides smuggling narcotics and people across the US-Mexico border. But are they criminals threatening the safety of local communities or victims of child trafficking?

Unaccompanied child migrants from Central America and Mexico arriving at the US southern border first became national news in the summer of 2014. A multitude of front-page stories about the influx of unaccompanied children and youth traveling to the United States from Honduras, Guatemala, El Salvador, and Mexico to seek refuge

E. M. Goździak, *Human Trafficking as a New (In)Security Threat*,
https://doi.org/10.1007/978-3-030-62873-4_6

from horrific violence—rape, gang recruitment, and murder—followed (Blume 2014; Constable 2014; Frelick 2014; Strain 2014; Terrio 2014). Advocacy groups and UN agencies produced reports urging international protection for the children on the move (CGRS 2014; UNHCR 2014). Migration policy advisors and congressional researchers also chimed in (Ryan 2014; Seghetti et al. 2014). The attention overwhelmingly centered on the push factors driving the arrival of unaccompanied children and youth to the United States and their treatment while in government custody.

I, too, wrote about the young Central Americans. I focused on those who were released to family and community. I tried to answer questions about their integration in local communities (Goździak 2015). In this chapter, I want to draw attention to unaccompanied adolescents—mainly males, but also some females—who fled violence and extreme poverty in their countries of origin, but also served as drug mules or foot guides smuggling narcotics and people across the US-Mexico border as this was often their only way to get to the United States.[1] Drawing on narratives elicited from the unaccompanied youths by law enforcement, social workers, and *pro bono* attorneys seeking immigration relief for these young people, I analyze the boys' and girls' involvement in criminal activities as well as their experiences at the hands of Mexican cartels and drug lords. I examine the narratives to answer a few fundamental questions: Are these young people juvenile criminals or victims of child trafficking? Should they be released to families and communities? Would their release jeopardize the safety and security of those communities? I use my interviews with federal officials to assess the unaccompanied adolescents' risk for deportation and prospects for immigration relief, but I don't stop there. I also explore what needs to be done for the children's long-term prosperity, well-being, and human security.

The data that informs this chapter come from narratives elicited from 50 children and adolescents over an 18-month period in 2015 and 2016. The majority of the minors were males (35); the remaining 15 were females. In many instances, I had access to 2–3 narratives, elicited at different times and by different people, per child. The narratives did not include the names or current whereabouts of the children, but did provide some basic demographic data. The youngsters hailed from Mexico (20), Guatemala (9), El Salvador (5), Honduras (3), Brazil (1), Ghana (2), and

[1] I focus on adolescents who arrived prior to the most recent humanitarian crisis at the US-Mexico border.

India (1). The Mexican, Guatemalan, Salvadoran, and Honduran adolescents were part of the Central American cohort of unaccompanied minors that began to arrive at the southern border of the United States in 2014 or earlier. Narratives obtained from an additional nine young people (2 females and 7 males) lacked information on country of origin.

In eight cases, there was also no information about the exact age of the individual. The vast majority of the young people were older adolescents: 23 were 17 years of age and 13 were 16 years old. Given the content of the narratives about the nine young people whose age was not included, I surmised that they too were teenagers, as references were made to them being placed in high school or working for several years. Only two children were 12 years of age or younger. Despite the preponderance of adolescents in the group, the press, child advocates, and the federal government referred to them as children.

Seventeen of the young people were involved in smuggling people across the US-Mexico border and eight smuggled drugs. Twenty-two of the adolescents experienced some form of labor exploitation and nine were exploited sexually. Eight admitted to abusing drugs.

I read and analyzed the narratives against the definition of severe forms of child trafficking enshrined in the TVPA of 2000. The TVPA of 2000, as amended, and accompanying federal criminal statutes define severe forms of trafficking in persons as:

- Sex trafficking in which…the person induced to perform a commercial sex act has not attained 18 years of age; or
- The recruitment, harboring, transportation, provision, or obtaining of a person for labor or services, through the use of *force*, *fraud*, or *coercion*, for the purpose of subjection to involuntary servitude, peonage, debt bondage, or slavery (emphasis added) (22 U.S.C. § 7102 (8)).

The law provides further clarifications and indicates that:

- Sex trafficking means "recruitment, harboring, transportation, provision or obtaining of a person for the purpose of a commercial sex act" (22 U.S.C. § 7102(9)).

- Commercial sex act means "any sex act on account of which anything of value is given to or received by any person" (22 U.S.C. § 7102(3)).
- Coercion means threats of serious harm to or physical restraint against any person; any scheme, plan, or pattern intended to cause a person to believe that failure to perform an act would result in serious harm to or physical restraint against any person; or the abuse or threatened abuse of the legal process (22 U.S.C. § 7102(2)).
- Involuntary Servitude "includes a condition of servitude induced by means of (A) any scheme, plan, or pattern intended to cause a person to believe that, if the person did not enter into or continue in such condition, that person or another person would suffer serious harm or physical restraint; or (B) the abuse or threatened abuse of the legal process" (22 U.S.C. § 7102(5)).
- Peonage means a status or condition of involuntary servitude based upon real or alleged indebtedness (8 CFR 214.11).
- Debt bondage means "the status or condition of a debtor arising from a pledge by the debtor of his or her personal services or of those of a person under his or her control as a security for debt, if the value of those services as reasonably assessed is not applied toward the liquidation of the debt or the length and nature of those services are not respectively limited and defined" (22 U.S.C. § 7102(4)).

Based on close reading of the narratives against this legal backdrop, I tried to ascertain whether the minor was a victim of severe forms of trafficking. In 29 of the 50 cases, I was certain that the minor met the definition. In 10 cases, the evidence suggested that the young person was not trafficked. In the remaining 11 cases, I was not able to make an informed decision based on the provided information. I will return to some of these cases later in this chapter to discuss the youngsters' experiences, including involvement in drug and/or people smuggling, violence at the hands of the drug cartels and traffickers, substance abuse, and different forms of exploitation.

Setting the Stage

The press portrayed the Central American children and youth who arrived at our southern border in 2014 as a migration phenomenon without precedence. Nothing can be further from the truth. Child migrants have been coming to America alone since Ellis Island. Annie Moore, a 15-year-old girl from Cork County, Ireland and her two younger brothers were the first persons in line on January 1, 1892, the opening day of the new immigration station at Ellis Island (Tanseem 2014).

Several waves of unaccompanied children have entered the United States since. From 1960 to 1962, Operation Pedro Pan (Peter Pan) resulted in the airlift from Cuba of what historians say were 14,000 unaccompanied children. It was one of the largest migrations of unaccompanied children into the United States from a single country. In 1975, Operation Baby Lift involved a mass evacuation of about 3,000 orphans from South Vietnam. Since 1980, almost 13,000 children and youth under the age of 18 have entered the unaccompanied refugee minors (URM) program, funded by the Office of Refugee Resettlement (ORR) and administered by the Lutheran Immigration and Refugee Services (LIRS) and the U.S. Conference of Catholic Bishops (USCCB). At its peak in 1985, ORR provided protection to 3,828 children. In 1982, Congress passed the Amerasian Homecoming Immigration Act, giving preferential immigration status to Vietnamese children born to US servicemen. About 23,000 Amerasians and 67,000 of their relatives entered the United States under this Act (Johnson 2002).

According to some researchers, over 100,000 children are apprehended every year entering the United States unaccompanied by parents or other legal guardians, and without valid immigration documents (Uehling 2008). A study by the National Autonomous University of Mexico indicates that an estimated 150,000 young people under the age of 18 attempt to cross the US border annually from Mexico. Approximately 60,000 are offered 'voluntary deportation' and return home immediately, but the rest are detained or disappear into the undocumented population (Thompson 2008).

The statistics on unaccompanied children and adolescents who have been crossing the southern border starting in 2013 are often confusing. Some reports include both Mexican and Central American youngsters, while some focus solely on Central Americans. The Pew Research Center, citing data obtained under the Freedom of Information Act (FOIA) from government sources, points out that that the number of unaccompanied children arriving between October 2013 and June 2014 reached 57,000, compared with nearly 39,000 in the previous fiscal year (FY 2012). The data cited by the Pew Research Center include both Central American (El Salvador, Honduras, Guatemala) and Mexican children (Krogstad et al.

2014). According to a UNHCR report, *Children on the Run*, since 2009 UNHCR has registered an increased number of asylum seekers, both children and adults, from El Salvador, Honduras, and Guatemala lodging claims in the Americas. Citing US Customs and Border Protection (CBP) sources, the report indicates that the total number of apprehensions of unaccompanied and separated children and youth arriving in the United States from these three countries jumped from 4,059 in FY 2011 to 10,443 in FY 2012 to 21,537 in FY 2013 (UNHCR 2014).

What sets the recently arrived youth apart from previous cohorts of young people, mainly adolescent males, searching for better opportunities in the United States? Available data suggest that the majority of unaccompanied minors in the care of the Office of Refugee Resettlement (ORR) for the past few years have indeed been above 14 years of age (86% in FY 2012 and 83% in FY 2011) and that the vast majority of them have been male (77% in FY 2012 and FY 2011, and 71% in FY 2010).[2] But there are some noteworthy changes in the gender patterns. The Pew Research Center points out that the number of unaccompanied females under the age of 18 apprehended at the border has increased significantly in recent years. In FY 2013, 7,339 females under the age of 18 were apprehended at the border, compared to 13,008 caught between October 1, 2013, and May 31, 2014. Four-in-ten of all unaccompanied children and youth apprehended in 2014 from Honduras (40%) and El Salvador (39%) are female, higher than the share among Guatemalans (24%). The vast majority of the unaccompanied females are teenagers between 13 and 17 years of age (Krogstad et al. 2014). According to interviews with advocates at the border, many of these teens are young mothers. Chronologically—at least by Western standards—they are children, but in terms of self-identity they are mothers with adult responsibilities.

A report prepared by scholars from the American University underscores the nationality of the young migrants. Of the more than 68,000 unaccompanied children apprehended in FY 2014, 51,705 (or 75%) are from the "Northern Triangle" countries of Central America: El Salvador, Guatemala, and Honduras. The number of unaccompanied children from these countries has increased 15-fold over the past five years (Stinchcomb and Hershberg 2014).

[2] Author's calculations from US Department of Health and Human Services, Office of Refugee Resettlement "Reports to Congress FY 2010-2014," 2010–2014.

Some service providers believe that the label 'unaccompanied children' is misleading. While the majority of the children and youth arriving from Central America cross the border unaccompanied, many are fairly quickly reunited with family (parents, uncles/aunts, adult siblings) or community members. Calling them unaccompanied post-release may not accurately describe their situation.[3] Indeed, ORR (2014) has indicated that they had released 53,518 unaccompanied children and youth to family and community members between October 1, 2013, and September 30, 2014 (FY 2014) and an additional 3,310 in FY 2015 (October 1, 2014–January 22, 2015). By releasing these young people to family and community ORR *de facto* abdicates the custody and responsibility to care for them, which makes the youngsters dependent on their sponsors and possibly vulnerable to abuse.

Over the years, unaccompanied children included refugees who fled wars and ethnic cleansing and young people from poverty-stricken countries searching for decent livelihoods and educational opportunities. What distinguishes the group of Mexican and Central American youths from previous cohorts of unaccompanied minors is their involvement in criminal activities. While many unaccompanied children violated US immigration laws, crossing borders illegally and remaining in the country without authorization are considered misdemeanors requiring civil—not criminal—penalties. Drug trafficking[4] and people smuggling,[5] on the other hand, are criminal offenses. Several questions, however, remain: Did these young people commit these criminal acts of their own volition or were they forced to commit these crimes? And if they were forced, are they therefore victims of child trafficking? And more importantly, what are their prospects for the future: deportation, detention, immigration relief, successful integration into the United States?

[3] Kristyn Peck, at the time Deputy Director of Children's Services at USCCB. Personal communication October 2014.

[4] See Title 18, Section 545 of the US Criminal Code.

[5] See US Immigration and Nationality Act. (I.N.A.), including Sections 274(a)(1)(a) and 274(a)(2).

Escaping Violence to Fall Prey to Violence

Migrants from Mexico and the northern triangle of Central America (Honduras, Guatemala, and El Salvador) have long fled poverty to seek better livelihoods in the United States. However, in recent years Central American and Mexican migrants, including underage children, also flee widespread violence that, according to some, reaches civil war levels. El Salvador became the most violent country in the western hemisphere in 2015 with a murder rate of 103 per 100,000 persons, while Honduras suffered 57 violent murders per 100,000, and Guatemala 30 per 100,000 people (Speck 2016).

In their study *Children on the Run*, UNHCR indicates that 38% of the children they studied ($N = 404$), fell prey to recruitment into and exploitation by the criminal industry of human smuggling. Eleven percent of the children reported having suffered from or being in fear of both violence in society and abuse in the home. All of the children and adolescents in my study witnessed, experienced, or have been threatened with violence. Thirteen boys and two girls suffered violence at the hands of gang or cartel members.

Marisa[6] reported that when she was 13 years old, she and her friend were kidnapped by members of *Cartel del Gulfo*. The cartel members held the girls for about a week when a Mexican policeman who collaborated with the cartel told them that they had the wrong girls. Marisa and her friend were let go. At the age of 15, Mario and his best buddy were kidnapped under the cover of dark by armed men a block from Mario's home in Veracruz, Mexico. The men put plastic bags over the boys' heads, forced them to lay down on the floor of a pick-up truck, and took them to see the *Comandante*. Surrounded by several armed men, the *Comandante* told Mario and his friend that they would have to work as foot guides and that any attempt to escape would result in the death of their mothers. In some cases, the cartels started recruiting children as young as 10 or 11 years old. Alejandro, a Mexican street child, was 11 years old when gang members wrapped him in a blanket and snatched him from the street to turn him into their errand boy. A few months later the cartel forced him to deliver drugs across the border and beat him when he refused. Alejandro believed that the cartel would murder him if he did not comply.

[6] All names of individuals and places are pseudonyms.

Citing Juan Pablo Perez Saintz (2014), Stinchomb and Hershberg indicate that Central American children and adolescents "are unable to find refuge from violence even at home. The domestic sphere, typically considered a protective space amid rampant insecurity in these communities, has also become a stage for violence resulting from the process of social exclusion (…)—lack of employment opportunities and basic state services" (Perez Saintz 2014: 21). I am not convinced that frustration stemming from inability to provide for the livelihoods of families causes domestic violence, but it certainly can exacerbate aggressive behavior of the perpetrators.

Seven children (three girls and four boys) experienced violence at the hands of their family members or caretakers, including beatings if they did not want to work and turn over earnings to the adults with whom they lived. Analisa, a girl from Guatemala, was abandoned by her biological parents when she was very little and was raised by a non-kin couple, whom she nevertheless called auntie and uncle. She worked for the couple both in and outside the home, cooking, washing dishes, doing laundry, tending a coffee plot, and selling the coffee at the market. If her work was not up to his standards, her 'uncle' would pull her hair, throw her against a wall, hit her, and dump hot food on her head. He also made sexual advances toward Analisa; he would come into her bedroom and would also watch her while she was showering.

There was a brothel in the town where Analisa lived. The Madam tried to recruit Analisa to work for her and her male partner. She tried to lure Analisa with promises of good money and nice clothes. The memory of being raped by several unknown men when she was 12 years old and a suicide of her friend who worked as a sex worker made Analisa resolve to never succumb to the woman's offer. In the end, Analisa ran away from her caretakers' home to try to go to the United States.

Migrants escaping violence at home fall prey to violence *en rout*e to the United States. While the journey north from Central America had always been treacherous and costly, in recent years it has become deadlier and pricier than ever, said the representatives of the binational Kino Border Initiative, Fathers Ricardo Machuca and Sean Carroll (Dickinson 2014). The "Mexican drug cartels have identified a lucrative niche of opportunity in the geostrategic position of Mexico as 'bridge country' for migration flows towards the U.S., and are now actively exploiting it" (Davilla 2015). *Los Zetas*, *Sinaloa*, and *Knights of Templar* cartels (Dickinson 2014) have formed alliances with gangs such as *Mara Salvatrucha* or MS-13 as well as

Calle 18 to protect or escort *transportistas* or drug smuggling specialists (Farah 2012) and are currently controlling the US-Mexico border and the routes leading up to it from the Northern Triangle (Honduras, El Salvador, and Guatemala) countries. They have de facto turned "what was once a relatively informal and somewhat familial underground operation into a highly sophisticated human trafficking network" (Dickinson 2014).

Some of the youth came to the United States by paying an old-fashioned *coyote*—usually with borrowed money—and being smuggled across the frontier. In some instances, they had to work to pay off at least part of the debt before they embarked on the journey north. Rosa Maria's mother borrowed the money needed to pay a *coyote* from her relative whose husband owned a large ranch and watermelon farm in Mexico. The 14-year-old Rosa Maria and her brothers, Juan and Carlos, toiled from dawn to dusk on their uncle's ranch. Rosa Maria prepared meals for the entire family and several farmhands, washed clothes, and cleaned the house. Juan mowed the lawn and kept the outside tidy while Carlos worked in the watermelon fields. Before their mother departed for the United States, Rosa Maria and her brothers worked hard, but were not mistreated. After their mom's departure, their aunt increased their workload and refused to provide them with food and clothing. She also threatened to hand the children over to the *coyote* who, she said, would either kill or kidnap them to extort money from their mother.

In many more instances, gangs and cartels facilitated the crossing of the US border. Cartel members told several boys and girls that they could pay for their own journey across the US southern border by serving as foot guides to smuggle other people or by trafficking drugs. Many more boys (13) than girls (4) were involved in smuggling people. Eight boys smuggled drugs; some smuggled both people and narcotics.

Marisa paid a guide to help her go to the United States. Marisa reported that she was traveling with a group of people when the guide abandoned them. Somehow the group crossed the border safely and Marisa went to live with a friend of hers in Arizona. However, after a few months, Marisa decided to return to Mexico. Upon returning to her hometown, Marisa was approached by a cartel about guiding small groups of people into the United States. Marisa told her attorney that she did not want to serve as a foot guide, but was aware that people who did not comply with the cartel's requests died. In the end, she smuggled people across the US southern border several times. In one interview, she said she made seven attempts to cross the border, but was successful only on two occasions.

Jorge, a 17-year old from Mexico, worked as a *coyote* for several months and made 55 trips across the border before he was apprehended. He received $100 for each individual he crossed. Jorge reported that typically he smuggled about 10 individuals at a time. Because of his success, he was approached by a different gang to start working for them. Jorge refused, but the gang leader grabbed Jorge by his shoulders, forced him into a truck, took him to a river, and told him to cross six immigrants on an inflatable device. The trip ended in an apprehension.

Many of the adolescents were not as lucky as Jorge. Some of the boys and girls have been apprehended several times, but continued to be forced to cross people or drugs to the United States. Maria was apprehended by immigration twice, first at the border and later at her place of employment. Immigration and Customs Enforcement (ICE) officers identified her as "an immigrant minor who was not compliant with going to court after being released from her UAC (Unaccompanied Alien Children) placement." Maria said she had not received the mailed notification to appear in court because of disputes with her cousin's landlord.

Marisa said she heard that some of the US immigration officers were colluding with the smugglers. She said she witnessed immigration officers pay members of the cartel large sums of money for a police dog that was captured by the cartel. She also indicated that *la migra* threatened to beat her with a plank of wood during her most recent apprehension. It is unclear if Marisa was telling the truth. Her social worker noted that Marisa exhibited symptoms of paranoia and mood swings and it was often difficult to discern between what really happened to her and the narratives she produced.

Multiple Placements in Care

Under the William Wilberforce Trafficking Victims Protection Reauthorization Act (TVPRA) of 2008, unaccompanied minors from non-contiguous countries such as the Northern Triangle countries apprehended at the border are transferred within 72 hours to the Office of Refugee Resettlement (ORR) in the US Department of Health and Human Services. Under the TVPRA, this transfer of custody happens irrespective of whether the minor meets the credible fear standard or may be eligible for immigration relief as a victim of trafficking or other qualifying crimes (Stinchomb and Hershberg 2014). Taking into consideration the child's best interest and security, ORR placed the child in one of four detention settings: shelter care, staff-secure care, secure-care or short-term foster care. Most unaccompanied children spend, on average, 35 days in HHS custody (DHHS Fact Sheet). The vast majority have been released to family or community. Mark Greenberg, Acting Assistant Secretary in the Administration for Children and Families (ACF), testified that in FY 2014, "approximately 95% of children were released to a parent, relative, or non-relative sponsor" (Greenberg 2014).

However, as unaccompanied children and adolescents await release to family or community members, it is not unusual that they switch placements. In fact, nine boys in my study changed placements several times: four changed placements as many as six times, three were transferred to different facilities three times, and the remaining two were placed in two different programs. According to Kristyn Peck, a former Director of Children's Services at the US Conference of Catholic Bishops (USCCB), there are lots of reasons for changes in placements. "If ORR determines a child has a 'quick' reunification case, they are likely to request transfer to one of the large facilities ORR subcontracts from the Department of Defense, where they expect a short stay before discharge. This frees up traditional bed space for kids who may need a home study or will otherwise be in care longer," said Kristyn. Youth who do not have family reunification cases may be transferred to long-term foster care, with the expectation that they will become eligible for the Unaccompanied Refugee Minor (URM) program, and be able to stay in the same placement, she added (personal communication, March 2017). All of USCCB long-term foster care placements are also URM sites.

In the case of male adolescents, they are more likely to be sent to secure or staff-secure settings if they have criminal histories, even if the 'criminal' activity was conducted through force or coercion by a trafficker. Then, if they are 'stepped down' into a less restrictive setting for good behavior, that would be another change in placement. The reverse is also true, youth may also be 'stepped up' to a more restrictive placement due to significant behavioral challenges, serious mental health needs, history of substance abuse, or if they are perceived to be 'run risk.' There is no research on the effects of these multiple placements on the young people's well-being.

Legal Outcomes and Long-Term Solutions

The Homeland Security Act of 2002 stipulates that the Office of Refugee Resettlement (ORR) develop a plan for children in their custody to have access to legal representation. Legal representation is critical to any immigration relief—asylum, Special Juvenile Status (SJS), and T- or U-visas—the children might be granted. Research shows that 90% of children appearing in immigration courts without an attorney were ordered to leave the United States; 77% through removal orders and 13% via voluntary departure. Represented by an attorney, children's odds of remaining in the United States increased from 10% to nearly 50% (Stinchomb and Hershberg 2014).

At the time I conducted this analysis, the Office on Trafficking in Persons (OTIP) in the federal government was not able to provide data on final dispositions on the 50 cases I examined; some of the cases were still pending. They did, however, indicate that close to 90% of the cases they review have a positive resolution: the vast majority of the children and adolescents are deemed to have been trafficked, despite engaging in criminal activities, and get T-Visas that provide them with eligibility for several months of services and *de facto* put them on a path to citizenship or are considered to have been abandoned by their families and get a Special Juvenile Status (SJS) that also allows them to remain in the country. This is a high percentage of approval. My own assessment was much lower. I concluded that about 58% of the cases I analyzed qualified to be considered trafficked children and youth under the current legislation.

I have always maintained that immigration relief is the most important aspect of immigrants'—children's and adults'—integration into the United States. I stand by this assertion in the case of unaccompanied children and adolescents. However, to ensure long-term prosperity, well-being, and human security these young people need assistance beyond an immigration visa. Some face serious challenges to successful integration.

First, debt. Without exception, all of the young people in this study or their family incurred debts. In many instances, these were not insignificant amounts of money and must be repaid. Juanita's aunt financed the 17-year-old Guatemalan's journey to the United States. She paid the *coyote* $2000 upfront and promised to give him an additional $2000 once Juanita arrived safely in Houston. Juanita was apprehended by Border Patrol, but in short order was released to her aunt who immediately put the girl to work to pay off the loan. Juanita works in a restaurant making approximately $55/day. Her aunt charges her $300/week for her debt and additional $400/month for room and board. There is not much left after these 'deductions.' Maria's father incurred a debt of 40,000 *quetzales* (about $5500) with a 10% interest accrual. Maria is having a hard time paying back the debt; so far, she has managed to send her parents only $700. The people Maria's father borrowed money from are threatening violence if the money does not get paid back soon. Flora's parents borrowed 26,000 *quetzales* from her cousin. They also gave her cousin some land as payment security. If Flora is unable to send money to her parents, they will lose their farm, the only source of livelihood they have.

Some service providers indicated that the debts could be paid off quicker if the sponsors the children live with charged them modest rent or allowed them to live in their homes free of charge, at least for a while. Child advocates indicated that they also worry that the trafficking networks reach far and might come to harm the young people. I worry that in order to make enough money to support themselves and to pay back the debts they incurred to come to the United States, the youngsters might undertake risky employment and be exploited again. Their security after release is indeed a very fragile state.

A few of the adolescent girls have already reported exploitation. Sixteen-year-old Flora said she felt obliged to work because she feared that her sponsor would abuse her—verbally or possibly physically—if she did not. At first, Flora worked alongside her sponsor from 4 to 8 pm—after coming back from school—cleaning houses, but later on she was expected to complete the work on her own. She makes approximately $1000 every two weeks, but Flora gets to keep only $300 despite the fact that she now works alone.

Carla hails from Honduras. She is a teen mother of a two-year-old daughter, Naya, and was released to her older brother, Alejandro, who paid $9,000 for Carla and Naya to be smuggled to the United States. Alejandro charges Carla $250/month for rent and $80/week for babysitting. Carla goes to school and works about 30 hours a week in a local grocery store stocking foodstuffs. She makes $230/week but after paying rent and babysitting, she has little money left. Alejandro does not share meals with his sister and Carla has to buy food for herself and Naya. She spends approximately $30–40/week on groceries. There is nothing left from her salary to start paying off her smuggling debt. Alejandro is often angry at Carla and takes his frustration out on his niece as well.

Carla reported that he hit Naya several times either with a belt or his bare hand, leaving bruises.

Second, substance abuse. Several children reported substance abuse. It was not uncommon for some of the children to start taking drugs at a young age. According to her mother, Marisa started taking drugs when she turned 12 years old. Marisa's mother indicated that Marisa had access to drugs through her boyfriend who was a member of *Los Zetas*. However, both Marisa and Christian denied any involvement with the cartel. Nevertheless, at least one of the narratives I read suggested Marisa was taking drugs both in Mexico and in the United States. Marisa admitted that at one point she was so addicted that she "would consume cocaine and crystal all day if available." Marisa's mother placed her daughter in a rehab twice, but is not very hopeful that the girl will not relapse. Marisa told her social worker that the rehab staff mistreated her. She claimed she was tied up and was fed "rotten food."

Juan said that his father offered him his first beer at the age of four. At the age of six, Juan broke his leg and instead of taking him to the doctor, his parents kicked him out of the house. The boy spent time in the streets and slept under bridges. He began using marijuana on a daily basis at the age of 10 to dull the pain stemming from the broken bones and abandonment by his parents. Juan also said that he regularly used *Revotril* pills and inhaled spray cans, along with using ecstasy and cocaine. One day under the influence of pills, Juan grabbed a knife and tried to stab his friend, but upon reflection threw the knife away and ran. A member of *El Cartel del Gulfo* found Juan, pushed him against a car and hit him on the head multiple times with a radio, and ripped off his eyebrow ring.

Seven boys talked about being forced to take drugs by the traffickers who sent them across the border with backpacks full of marijuana, cocaine, and other substances. 'Drug parties' were often part of the initiation process to become a food guide or a drug trafficker.

Third, mental health and behavioral problems. If violence is one of the major push factors propelling Central American youth to leave their homelands, integration efforts need to consider the effects of witnessing violence, being a victim of violence, and perpetrating violence on the well-being of the children and youth and devise means to address those effects. Ruiz reported that during one of his journeys across the border he learnt that his grandmother who raised him from infancy died. Apparently, Ruiz has always felt sad and hopeless, but upon hearing the news about his beloved *abuelita* he started hearing voices telling him to kill himself. Ruiz was transferred to a psychiatric hospital and prescribed drugs for his depression. The narratives were silent on how he was doing on the psychotropic drugs.

Looking Forward

The decisions that the federal government has made regarding the unaccompanied children's and adolescents' immigration status have been part of what scholars are conceptualizing as 'humanitarianism at home' (see Ticktin 2011; also Redfield and Bornstein 2011) that contrasts our notions of humanitarianism that have always focused on involvement of actors from Western nations in disadvantaged countries around the globe. The treatment of the unaccompanied children by the US federal government is an example of humanitarian efforts carried out "at home," by the government within the territory of the nation-state. The high rates of immigration relief also speak volumes about exercising humanitarian action and about the "politics of compassion" (Uehling 2008).

When children cross borders, they are caught in divergent processes, as the state both criminalizes them as foreigners—and, in this particular case, as smugglers of people and drugs—and aims to protect their well-being specifically as children (Terrio 2015; Uehling 2008). Yet, as Fassin outlines: "Criminalization and humanitarianism do not simply function as alternative policies. They often operate in a dialectical way" (Fassin 2013: 50). This "combination of repression and compassion" (Fassin 2013: 50) creates an "empire of humanitarianism" (Fassin 2013: 49), one in which state power can become a primary channel for constructing criminals and "doing good."

The government and their outside consultants closely scrutinized the criminal actions of the boys and girls who smuggled people and drugs in order to assess the credibility of the youngsters' assertions that they have been victims of trafficking. In the end, the government deemed most of them to be victimized and therefore not responsible for the criminal actions, because they were children who could not consent to smuggling people and drugs. However, the young people faced certain challenges. The state created what Agamben (2005) calls spaces of exception, i.e., the increase of power structures the government employs in supposed times of crisis. Within these times of crisis, Agamben refers to increased extension of power as states of exception, where questions of citizenship and individual rights can be diminished, superseded, and rejected in the process of claiming this extension of power by a government. In the case of the apprehended children and youth, the government created spaces of exception during the apprehension and rescue at the nation's borders as well as throughout the process of detention or protective custody. As indicated above, there is limited research on the effects of detention on undocumented children and youth (Terrio 2015; Heidbrink 2014), especially on the cohort of youth engaged in criminal activity.

The question that still remains is: Will the desire to 'do good' and show compassion extend beyond the immigration relief? As indicated above, upon releasing these boys and girls to family and community members, ORR abdicated their custody of the young people. Granted, many of those released to family are eligible for limited social services, but will the fear of deportation prevent them from accessing these services? Moreover, are the services appropriate to rehabilitate young people who have experienced violence and have been forced to commit criminal acts?

References

Agamben, Giorgio. 2005. *The State of Exception*, trans. Kevin Attell. Chicago: University of Chicago Press.

Blume, Howard. 2014. LAUSD Opens Doors to Young Central American Immigrants. *LA Times*, August 13.

Center for Gender and Refugee Studies, Kids in Need of Defense (KIND). 2014. A Treacherous Journey: Child Migrants Navigating the U.S. Immigration System. San Francisco and Washington, DC. http://cgrs.uchastings.edu/our-work/treacherous-journey.

Constable, Pamela. 2014. Maryland, Virginia Suburbs Receive Surge of Border Kids from Central America. *Washington Post*, August 27.

Davilla, Ana. 2015. Drug Cartels: Where Human Trafficking and Human Smuggling Meet Today. *The Huffington Post* The Blog, June 16. http://www.huffingtonpost.com/ana-davila/drug-cartels-where-human-trafficking-and-human-smuggling-meet-today_b_7588408.html.

Dickinson, Caitlin. 2014. How Mexico's Cartels Are Behind the Border Kid Crisis. *The Daily Beast*, September 7.

Farah, Douglas. 2012. Central American Gangs: Changing Nature and New Partners. *Journal of International Affairs* 66 (1) (Fall/Winter): 53–67.

Fassin, Didier. 2005. Compassion and Repression. The Moral Economy of Immigration Policies in France. *Cultural Anthropology* 20 (3): 362–387.

Fassin, Didier. 2013. *Enforcing Order: An Ethnography of Urban Policing*. Polity.

Frelick, Bill. 2014. Are Central American Kids the New Boat People? *Politico*. August 13.

Goździak, Elżbieta M. 2015. What Kind of Welcome? Integration of Central American Unaccompanied Children into Local Communities. Washington, DC.

Greenberg, Mark. 2014. Statement by Mark Greenberg Acting Assistant Secretary Administration for Children and Families U.S. Department of Health and Human Services Before the Committee on Homeland Security and Governmental Affairs. United States Senate, July 9.

Heidbrink, Lauren. 2014. *Migrant Youth, Transnational Families, and the State Care and Contested Interests*. University of Pennsylvania Press.

Johnson, Kay. 2002. Children of the Dust. *Time Magazine*, May 13.

Krogstad, Jens Manuel, Ana Gonzalez-Barrera, and Mark Hugo Lopez. 2014. At the Border, a Sharp Rise in Unaccompanied Girls Fleeing Honduras. Pew Research Center. http://www.pewresearch.org/fact-tank/2014/07/25/at-the-border-a-sharp-rise-in-unaccompanied-girls-fleeing-honduras/.

Nakamura, David. 2019. "Trump says the border crisis is about criminals and gangs. His administration says it is about families and children." *The Washington Post* May 2, 2019. Available at: https://www.washingtonpost.com/politics/trump-says-the-border-crisis-is-about-criminals-and-gangs-his-administration-says-it-is-about-families-and-children/2019/05/01/0f94d78c-6c37-11e9-8f44-e8d8bb1df986_story.html.

Office of Refugee Resettlement, US Department of Health and Human Services. 2014. Unaccompanied Children Released to Sponsors by State. https://www.acf.hhs.gov/orr/programs/ucs/state-by-state-uc-placed-sponsors.

Perez Saintz, Juan Pablo. 2014. Social Exclusion and Societal Violence: The Household Dimension. AULA Blog, March 6.

Redfield, Peter, and Erica Bornstein. 2011. An Introduction to the Anthropology of Humanitarianism. In *Forces of Compassion: Humanitarianism Between Ethics and Politics*, ed. Erica Bornstein and Peter Redfield. Santa Fe, NM: SAR Press.

Ryan, Kelly. 2014. Unaccompanied and Separated Minors: A Call for a Multidisciplinary Response to a Humanitarian Crisis. *Migration Policy and Practice* 4 (3) (July–September).

Seghetti, Lisa, Alison Siskin, and Ruth Ellen Wasem. 2014. Unaccompanied Alien Children: An Overview. Congressional Research Service, June 23.

Speck, Mary. 2016. Easy Pray: Criminal Violence and Central American Migration. Report No 57, July 28. Available at https://www.crisisgroup.org/latin-america-caribbean/central-america/easy-prey-criminal-violence-and-central-american-migration.

Stinchcomb, Dennis, and Eric Hershberg. 2014. *Unaccompanied Migrant Children from Central America. Context, Causes, and Responses*. Washington, DC: Center for Latin American and Latino Studies, American University.

Strain, Michael R. 2014. The Problem Isn't Central America's Child Refugees. It's the Countries They Come from. *Washington Post*, August 1.

Tasneem, Raja. 2014. Child Migrants Have Been Coming to America Since Ellis Island. Mother Jones Friday, July 18. http://www.motherjones.com/politics/2014/07/child-migrant-ellis-island-history.

Terrio, Susan, J. 2014. 'Life Ended There,' Rare Interviews with Children of America's Border Disaster. *Politico*, July 10.

Terrio, Susan J. 2015. *Whose Child Am I? Unaccompanied, Undocumented Children in U.S. Immigration Custody*. Berkeley: University of California Press.

Thompson, Amy. 2008. A Child Alone and Without Papers. A Report on the Return and Repatriation of Undocumented Children by the United States. Austin, TX: Center for Public Policy Priorities.

Ticktin, Miriam. 2011. *Casualties of Care. Immigration and the Politics of Humanitarianism in France*. Berkeley, CA: University of California Press.

Uehling, Greta L. 2008. The International Smuggling of Children: Coyotes, Snakeheads, and the Politics of Compassion. *Anthropological Quarterly* 81: 833–871. https://doi.org/10.1353/anq.0.0031.

UNHCR. 2014. Children on the Run. Unaccompanied Children Leaving Central America and Mexico and the Need for International Protection. Washington, DC. http://unhcrwashington.org/children.

U.S. Department of Health and Human Services, Office of Administration for Children and Families. Fact Sheet: U.S. Department of Human Services, Administration for Children and Families, Office of Refugee Resettlement, Unaccompanied Alien Children Program. https://www.acf.hhs.gov/sites/default/files/orr/unaccompanied_childrens_services_fact_sheet.pdf.

CHAPTER 7

Young and Male Asylum Seekers: A Security Threat to the European Union?

In the summer of 2015, pictures of Aylan Kurdi, a three-year-old Syrian boy who drowned as his family was forced to flee the city of Kobani to seek safe haven in Europe, pulled at the heartstrings of the global public (Ensor and Goździak 2016). The image, at least initially, evoked compassion and empathy, and increased support for liberal refugee policies across ideological divides (Sohlberg et al. 2019).

Children and women often dominate public imaginaries about asylum seekers and refugees. Refugee advocates for decades have argued that 'three-quarters of the world's refugees are women and children.' This mantra has been ingrained in the public psyche and invoked on many occasions to elicit compassion, grant asylum, and provide assistance to refugees. However, when a record 1.3 million refugees applied for asylum in the 28 member states of the European Union, Norway, and Switzerland in 2015 (Connor and Krogstad 2016), the reception of and attitudes toward those seeking safe haven was not always welcoming. The lack of compassion was partially driven by the demographic profile of the refugees, the majority of whom were young men.

According to the Pew Research, the asylum seekers arriving in Europe since 2013 have been mainly male and young. In 2013, 67% of asylum seekers arriving on Europe's doorsteps were male. This trend continued in 2014 and 2015 with 71 and 73% males, respectively. In all three years, 80–83% of the men were under 35 years of age. Also, in the same year

E. M. Goździak, *Human Trafficking as a New (In)Security Threat*,
https://doi.org/10.1007/978-3-030-62873-4_7

four-in-ten (or 42%) asylum seekers were young adult males (18 to 34 years of age), only one-in-ten (or 11%) were young adult females in the same age bracket (Connor and Krogstad 2016; see also Hudson 2016).

These age and gender patterns are consistent across some of the largest asylum seeker groups, including those from Syria, Iraq, Iran, and Somalia. The large proportion of young males and a much smaller numbers of young adult women and female children indicate that many refugees from these source countries are indeed young men traveling alone. The demographic profile of asylum seekers in destination countries also includes a large share of young adult men. In 2015, 71% of all asylum seekers to Sweden and 40% of asylum seekers to Germany were young adult males. In Hungary, 51% were young and male. Young adult men made up 74% of asylum seekers in Italy, the highest share of any country in 2015 (Connor and Krogstad 2016).

This demographic profile is not surprising given the fact that young men leaving countries like Afghanistan, Iraq, and Syria are quite vulnerable as they are often seen as potential combatants. This means that "even if a man does not have weapons and is not engaged in fighting, he is assumed at the very least to be willing to fight". He is therefore viewed either as an asset or as a threat—to the regime, the opposition movements, or the governments of host countries (Davis et al. 2014: 35).

The asylum seekers also included significant numbers of children and adolescents under the age of 18. In 2015, about two-in-ten (or 19%) of all asylum seekers were male minors (0 to 17 years of age). In comparison, female minors numbered one-in-ten (Connor and Krogstad 2016). The International Organization for Migration (IOM) estimated that more than half of those minors traveled to Europe as unaccompanied minors and that 90% were males (Hudson 2016).

The presence of children and adolescents among the asylum seekers was not entirely surprising. Children have always constituted a significant proportion of the international refugee populations. According to Jacqueline Bhabha (2004), the largest number of child refugees travel as members of families forced to flee persecution. Prior to the recent 'refugee crisis' in Europe, unaccompanied refugee minors comprised a much smaller number of refugee populations, approximately two to five percent. However, in 2015, the percentage of unaccompanied minors among all asylum seekers to Europe was much larger. According to Eurostat, between 2008 and 2016, about 198,500 unaccompanied minors have entered Europe seeking asylum. The first significant increase occurred in 2014, when the number of unaccompanied minors seeking asylum almost doubled compared with 2013, from 13,800 to 23,200. In 2015, the total quadrupled and reached 96,000 young individuals. Nearly seven percent of all first-time asylum applications in 2015 were from unaccompanied minors, the highest share since data on accompanied minors became available in 2008. Between 2008 and 2015, about 70 to 80% of these unaccompanied minors annually were boys ages 14 to 17. About 10% annually were girls in the same age cohort. It is noteworthy that most of these minors were older adolescents; only about 10% were children under 13 years of age (Connor and Krogstad 2016).

When governments debated how many migrants to accept onto their shores, they did consider gender balance. As Valerie Hudson (2016), a professor at Texas A&M University, wrote in *Politico*: "That might sound sexist on the surface, but years of research has shown that male-dominated societies are less stable, because they are more susceptible to higher levels of violence, insurgence and mistreatment of women." Societies with extremely skewed sex ratios are more unstable even without jihadi ideologues in their midst, claimed Deborah Den Boer and Valerie Hudson (2002). In their book *Bare Branches*, they analyzed the link between sex ratios and the emergence of both violent criminal gangs and anti-government movements. It makes sense, they argued, that when young males are marginalized their grievances are aggravated (Hudson and Den Boer 2005). The anthropologist Barbara Miller has persuasively argued that a normal sex ratio is a 'public good' and therefore deserves state protection (Miller 2001). These arguments suggest that for any European country to wind up with a skewed adult sex ratio would be a tragedy for European men and women alike. From a purely demographic perspective these are sound arguments. However, they are rarely brought up in relation to non-immigrant populations. Is it a coincidence or deliberate discrimination?

When a large number of German women were attacked in several cities on New Year's Eve in 2015 by men whom the authorities describe as of 'North African or Arabic' descent, policy-makers sounded alarms about the risks associated with a male-dominated migration. In the aftermath of the attacks, Germany passed strict sexual assault laws, including a provision to deport refugees if they are convicted in sex-assault cases. Refugee activists and advocates harshly criticized this aspect of the law (Noack 2016). It seems that seeing black or brown males policy-makers immediately assume that they must be refugees or migrants while in fact in many instances these are children and grandchildren of immigrants, born in Europe, often enjoying European citizenship.

These assumptions based on skin color and ethnicity are nothing new. I am reminded of the week Paris was burning when riots broke out in early November 2005 in France. Many wondered who were those rioters. Many were children and grandchildren of non-European immigrants. They were born in France, had French citizenship and French passports, but the French still called them 'immigrants' (Goździak 2006). For the most part, they were not observant Muslims and the riots were not a response to perceived attacks on Islam or a reflection of their cultural alienation from mainstream French society. The emphasis on cultural differences "downplay[ed] the more significant factors of economic marginalization, spatial segregation and anti-immigrant racism" (Terrio 2006: 4).

It is important to remember both the age and gender of the boys and men when we discuss attitudes toward asylum seekers. Small children evoke compassion, adolescent males not so much. When the adolescent and young adult males knocked on Europe's door to seek asylum, many Europeans saw them as cowards who should have stayed home to fight for their countries. Their gender and age squarely placed them in the public imaginaries as potential soldiers, not as children and young people deserving protection. Small children migrating without parents are considered to be trafficked, adolescent males are regarded as illegal migrants.

I have written extensively about attitudes toward refugees and anti-immigration policies, especially in Hungary and in Poland, elsewhere (Goździak and Márton 2018; Goździak 2019). However, it is worthwhile to examine again the kind of fear these young men aroused in Europeans and the kind of threat they were accused of posing to European societies.

Representations of 'Crisis'

The media and political discourses framed the arrival of asylum seekers in Europe in 2015 as a crisis (see Holmes and Castañeda 2016; Zunes 2017; Goździak et al. 2020). There is no denying that large numbers of asylum seekers and migrants reached Europe in recent years. According to the UN High Commissioner for Refugees (UNHCR), in 2015 alone, over one million asylum seekers were registered. More than 800,000 of them were smuggled by sea from Turkey to Greece, and the majority continued to travel through Europe to reach Germany and Sweden. In 2016, an estimated 362,000 refugees and migrants risked their lives crossing the Mediterranean Sea, with 181,400 people arriving in Italy, and 173,450 in Greece. In subsequent years, the numbers decreased, but refugees continue to seek safe haven in Europe to this day (Goździak et al. 2020).

These are indeed large numbers but do they constitute a 'crisis'? Is it warranted to use metaphors such as 'flood' or 'tide' to give an impression of a large-scale natural disaster? (see Holmes and Castañeda 2016; Hage 2016). Today's exodus from the Middle East pales in comparison with the situation Germany faced, and surmounted, after World War II. At the end of World War II, there were some 11 million displaced people in Germany alone. They were slave laborers, prisoners of war, and Holocaust survivors. The Germans who had lived in Eastern Europe were being expelled from Czechoslovakia, Poland, and Hungary. The arrival of several million newcomers in Europe in recent years presents real challenges, of course, but a prosperous European Union with a population in excess of 500 million has the means to overcome them, doesn't it?

In the late summer of 2019, 507 migrants and refugees were stranded on two rescue vessels, which picked them up of off the coast of Libya. UNHCR made an urgent appeal for the refugees to be allowed to disembark, calling it a 'race against time' as bad weather approached (Squires 2019). While some were trying to rescue refugees to avert a true crisis, others continued to propagate the crisis narrative.

'Crisis,' a concept which the Greeks used to delineate stark alternatives—right or wrong, salvation or damnation, life or death—has constantly framed modern ideas of history (Koselleck 2006). Migration scholars, however, argue that face-value acceptance of crisis narratives about asylum seekers coming to Europe in search of refuge results in viewing migration according to binary divisions: integration versus segregation, modernity versus cultural backwardness, the deserving versus the undeserving, and through the manufactured dichotomy between refugees and economic migrants (Crawley and Skleparis 2018; McMahon and Sigona 2018). In the context of our discussion of trafficking and security, the dichotomy also includes: trafficking versus smuggling, seeking protection versus posing a security threat.

Writing about the global refugee crisis, with a focus on Turkey, Jordan, and Lebanon as countries hosting large numbers of refugees, Sarah Kenyon Lischer rightly emphasizes that:

> Policy-makers often mistakenly view host state security and refugee security as unrelated–or even opposing–factors. In reality, refugee protection and state stability are linked together; undermining one factor weakens the other. Policies to protect refugees, both physically and legally, reduce potential threats from the crisis and bolster state security (Kenyon Lischer 2017: 85),

Cautionary lectures by migration scholars notwithstanding, politicians have certainly been exploiting the powerful narrative of 'crisis' as a political tactic. Sebastian Kurz, Victor Orbán, and Jarosław Kaczyński are but three politicians who have used the 'crisis' narrative to further their political causes. Kurz, the Federal Chancellor of Austria, invoked 'crisis' multiple times in an article published in *Time* magazine in 2017. He paired the word with phrases such as 'loss of control,' 'overwhelmed by developments,' 'a huge challenge for our country,' 'regain control,' and 'find solutions' (Kurz 2017).

Viktor Orbán, the Prime Minister of Hungary, has exploited the crisis narrative to defend his draconian measures aimed not only at barring refugees from Hungary, but also at criminalizing assistance to refugees and migrants. When some 400,000 mainly Muslim, refugees and asylum seekers crossed the Serbian-Hungarian border and descended on the Keleti Railway Station in Budapest in 2015, Viktor Orbán did not see the refugees fleeing war-torn countries as a humanitarian challenge but as a Muslim invasion that required an appropriate response: closing the Balkan land route to the European Union (Goździak and Márton 2018) and pressing the 'moral panic button' (Gerő and Sik 2020). His friend, Jarosław Kaczyński, the president of the Law and Justice party in Poland, has also been making the most of the crisis narrative despite the fact that, with the exception of some Chechens, there are virtually no refugees in Poland (Klaus 2020).

These crisis narratives went hand-in-hand with securitization of migration and the resulting perceptions that refugees and asylum seekers pose a serious threat to the security of transit countries and host societies.

Terrorism and Security Threat

Indeed, virtually every opinion poll on attitudes toward refugees indicates that many Europeans fear that refugees pose a major security threat to their country. Respondents assert that refugee communities harbor terrorists trafficked to Europe by organized crime groups. Although there is little substantive evidence linking refugees to recent terror attacks in Europe, surveys show the extent to which the connection between refugees and terrorism has figured in the public's mind (see Dempster and Hargrave 2017; Wike et al. 2016).

Security concerns are not only related to the refugees' gender, but also to their religion. In the public perception, the young males arriving in Europe are fighters and trouble makers not only because they are men but also because they are Muslim. Muslims are perceived to be jihadists. They are considered a security threat even in countries where there are very few Muslims. Researchers from the Pew Research Center found that most respondents in Poland, Greece, Hungary, Italy, and the United Kingdom agreed with the proposition that refugees posed a major threat to their country. Between 2014 and 2015, negative ratings for Muslims increased considerably in the United Kingdom (+9 percentage points), Spain (+8), Italy (+8), and Greece (+12). In France, where coordinated terrorist attacks by ISIS at the Bataclan concert hall and elsewhere in Paris in November, left 130 people dead, unfavorable opinions went up by +5 points in comparison with a previous year (Wike et al. 2016).

When large numbers of asylum seekers arrived in Hungary in 2015, Hungarian netizens lashed out at them. Many of those commenting on the arrival of asylum seekers have never seen and talked to refugees—or any other people—from the Middle East. Most of their 'information' came from a booklet *Forced settlement endangers our culture and traditions* distributed to 4.1 million Hungarian households. The 18-page booklet portrayed asylum seekers as dangerous to Europe's future. It linked migration to terrorism and referred to non-existent 'no-go zones' in European cities with large migrant populations, such as London, Paris, and Berlin, where authorities have allegedly lost control and where law and order were absent (Foundation Institute of Public Affairs 2018). Viktor Orbán and his government have not stopped at vilifying refugees. They also revamped a legislative proposal for a Russian-style civil society law that would have organizations aiding 'illegal migration' registered as foreign agents, subject to national security screening, and the confiscation of 25% of funds received from abroad (Than 2018).

Media, and to a certain extent the UN as well, depicted the arrival of Syrian refugees as the 'tip of the iceberg' (Kirka 2015). As securitization narratives emerged, refugees were increasingly portrayed as 'criminals' and 'terrorists.' Journalists described Syrian refugees as 'infiltrated with

Muslim extremists' and as an 'ISIS Trojan horse' (Holmes and Castañeda 2016). When a passport of a Syrian refugee was found near the body of the dead suicide bomber in the November 13, 2015 attacks in Paris, the fear of terrorism was palpable and many people believed that there was a connection between forced migrants and terrorists. A handful of jihadi terrorists did enter the Schengen Zone through Hungary, but the numbers were negligible. However, the Hungarian government systematically used the arrival of refugees as an opportunity to stigmatize refugees as terrorists (Goździak and Márton 2018). Antal Rogán, at the time leader of the Hungarian Fidesz' parliamentary group, warned of a future 'United European Caliphate,' while former Secretary of State László L. Simon urged Hungarians to make more babies in order to counter the negative cultural effects of mass migration such as the envisioned 'impending victory of Islamic parties imposing polygamy and destroying the remainder of European culture' (Simon 2015: 231). Beyond political statements, armed military police patrols on the streets of Budapest, in metro stations and in public spaces, have become a regular sight, as is the case in Paris and Brussels, while Hungary has yet to experience a terrorist attack.

Threat to the Christian Identity of Europe

The 2015 'refugee crisis' in Europe has resulted in public discussions about the threat that Muslim refugees pose to the Christian identity of the continent. The debates are especially fervent in the new accession countries in Central Europe. The expansion of the European Union (EU) eastwards meant an incorporation of countries whose values might not entirely align with the European 'norm.' What we are currently seeing in Europe is a need to balance the EU's security interests on the one hand and the interests of the development of democracy and the protection of human rights on the other.

It is interesting that in the increasingly secularized Europe, religion, paradoxically, has gained significance in many policy debates. Religious pluralism existed in Europe for centuries; in many countries quite unproblematically. However, the increasing religious (and ethnic) pluralism stemming from more recent migration resulted in challenges to religious freedom and religious tolerance, despite existing anti-discrimination laws (Pickel 2018). Even prior to the recent 'refugee crisis' debates about building mosques, wearing different forms of hijab, and providing religious education in schools abounded. This situation has changed even more dramatically in 2015. With the arrival of refugees from Syria and Afghanistan, governments and the general public started to link the refugees' identity to their religion (Pickel 2018; see also Koening 2005). Thus, refugees began to be equated with Muslims and Muslims with refugees. In extreme cases, refugees have been linked to Muslim fundamentalists.

In my own research on attitudes toward Muslim refugees, I analyzed, among others, comments posted by Poles on social media. Posts on londynek.net indicated Poles' deeply entrenched hatred of Muslims. The language used to describe Muslim immigrants in the United Kingdom, Germany, or Sweden was vulgar and racist. South Asians were often called 'ciapaci' (referring to the flatbread preferred by many Asians) or 'koziojebcy' (accusing Muslims of engaging in sexual intercourse with goats). References to stories about 'no-go-zones' in France or Sweden where Sharia laws prevail and disdain for local legal norms is, reportedly, paramount, abounded. The Catholic Poles zeroed in on the refugees' religion. They found Islam to be a threat. Opponents of admitting Muslim refugees suggested that Muslim men will rape Polish women and therefore must not be allowed to come to Poland. They also asserted that the Polish government and Polish men have a duty to protect their women from Muslim invaders (Goździak and Márton 2018; see also Goździak 2019).

The findings from my research were borne out by other studies. The Budapest-based Migration Research Institute carried out an opinion poll (Migrációkutató Intézet 2016) about attitudes to migrants, more specifically about what people think of cultural differences, of the security risks, and challenges associated with illegal migrants, and of the relation of illegal migrants and the situation of women and children. It is noteworthy that the opinion poll focused on 'illegal migration.' According to international human rights and refugee law, it is not illegal to seek asylum. Article 14 of the Universal Declaration of Human Rights asserts that everyone has the right to seek asylum from persecution. The United Nations 1951 Convention Relating to the Status of Refugees and the 1967 Protocol Relating to the Status of Refugees guide national legislation concerning political asylum. Under these agreements, a refugee is a person who is outside that person's own country's territory (or place of habitual residence if stateless) owing to fear of persecution on protected grounds, including race, caste, nationality, religion, political opinions, and membership in any particular social group or social activities. Rendering true victims of persecution to their persecutor is a violation of a principle called non-refoulement. Under these laws, all those seeking asylum were entitled to due process and an asylum hearing.

Yet, those expressing hostile attitudes toward refugees did not seem to care about existing laws. They took one look at pictures posted on the Internet or TV reports and decided that the young men were illegal migrants seeking better opportunities in Hungary and beyond. The opinion poll indicated that 79% of the respondents thought illegal migration represents a threat to women and children, while only 18% disagreed with the statement. Among the threats associated with migrants, terrorism was picked as the most significant potential risk by 28% of the respondents. Twenty-six percent of the survey respondents indicated increase of crime rates as a risk to the society at large. Fourteen percent said that illegal migrants increase the risk of violence against women and children, and 13% considered them a threat to Hungarian culture and identity. Respondents were less worried that migrants posed a threat to Hungarian citizens' job opportunities; only four percent worried about the economic impact of migration on the country's labor market. The survey also asked the respondents what they think about the compatibility of Muslim religion and Hungarian traditions. Eighty-four percent of the survey respondents said that the two are not compatible and the two religions and cultures cannot coexist. Similarly, 81% were convinced that migrants cannot integrate into European societies and economies (Migrációkutató Intézet 2016).

Fear of Small Numbers

In 2016, Europeans greatly overestimated the share of Muslims in the total population. The gap between perceptions and reality was even greater in 2020. Prior to the recent arrival of refugees in Europe in 2015, there were roughly 23 million Muslims living in the 28 European states. Three-quarters are European citizens either by birth or by naturalization. If we add to these numbers to the two million Muslims who recently sought refuge in Europe and have not yet been legalized, the number reaches 25 million Muslims. This accounts for about five percent of the total population of the continent (Khader 2016).

The perceptions, however, put the proportion of Muslims in Europe at a much higher level. According to international surveys conducted in 2016 and 2020, Europeans overestimated their country's Muslim population and the rate at which it is growing. German respondents guessed that more than one-fifth of the country's resident population was Muslim, while in reality it was less than five percent (Duncan 2016). According to the 2011 Hungarian Census, there were 5500 Muslims, mostly Sunni, living in Hungary (Wike et al. 2016). While large numbers of Muslim refugees transitioned through Hungary in 2015, very few received permission to stay, therefore the number of Muslims in Hungary continues to be negligible. Konrad Pędziwiatr (2015) estimates the number of Muslims in Poland to be between 25,000 and 40,000 people, while Grodź (2010) places the number within the range 15,000 to 30,000.

Do these relatively small numbers of Muslim refugees pose a security threat to the European continent? Or do policy-makers and the general public use them as an excuse to protect some imagined homogeneous Europe? There are no easy answers to these questions.

References

Bhabha, Jacqueline. 2004. Seeking Asylum Alone: Treatment of Separated and Trafficked Children in Need of Refugee Protection. *International Migration* 42 (1): 141–149.

Connor, Phillip, and Jens Manuel Krogstad. 2016. *Europe Sees Rise in Unaccompanied Minors Seeking Asylum, with Almost Half from Afghanistan*. Washington, DC: Pew Research Center. Available at: https://www.pewresearch.org/fact-tank/2016/05/10/eu-unaccompanied-minors/.

Crawley, Heaven, and Dimitris Skleparis. 2018. Refugees, Migrants, Neither, Both: Categorical Fetishism and the Politics of Bounding in Europe's "Migration Crisis". *Journal of Ethnic and Migration Studies* 44 (1): 48–64.

Davis, Rochelle, Abbie Taylor, and Emma Murphy. 2014. Gender, Conscription and Protection, and the War in Syria. *Forced Migration Review* 47: 35–38. Available at: https://www.fmreview.org/syria/davis-taylor-murphy.

Dempster, Helen, and Hargrave. 2017. Understanding Public Attitudes Towards Refugees and Migrants. Chatham House and ODI's Forum on Refugee and Migration Policy. Working Paper 512. Available at: https://euagenda.eu/upload/publications/untitled-92767-ea.pdf.

Den Boer, Andrea, and Valerie M. Hudson. 2002. A Surplus of Men, A Deficit of Peace: Security and Sex Ratios in Asia's Largest States. *Quarterly Journal: International Security* 26 (4): 5–39.

Duncan, Pamela. 2016. Europeans Greatly Overestimate Muslim Population, Poll Shows. *The Guardian*, December 13.

Ensor, Marisa O., and Elżbieta M. Goździak. 2016. Introduction: Durable Solutions During Transient Years. In *Children and Forced Migration: Durable Solutions During Transient Years*, ed. Marisa O. Ensor and Elżbieta M. Goździak, 1–21. New York: Palgrave Macmillan.

Foundation Institute of Public Affairs. 2018. *The Wages of Fear: Attitudes Towards Refugees and Migrants in Hungary*. Warsaw: Foundation Institute of Public Affairs.

Gerő, Márton, and Endre Sik. 2020. The Moral Panic Button: Construction and Consequences. In *Europe and the Refugee Response: A Crisis of Values?*, ed. Elżbieta M. Goździak, Izabella Main, and Brigitte Suter, 39–58. London: Routledge.

Goździak, Elżbieta M., Izabella Main, and Brigitte Suter (eds.). 2020. *Europe and the Refugee Response: A Crisis of Values?* London: Routledge.

Goździak, Elżbieta M. 2019. Using Fear of the "Other," Orbán Reshapes Migration Policy in a Hungary Built on Cultural Diversity. *Migration Information Source*, October 10.

Goździak, Elżbieta M., and Péter Márton. 2018. Where the Wild Things Are: Fear of Islam and the Anti-Refugee Rhetoric in Hungary and in Poland. *Central and Eastern European Migration Review* 7 (2): 125–151. https://doi.org/10.17467/ceemr.2018.04.

Goździak, Elżbieta M. 2006. The week Paris Was Burning. *Anthropology News*, January.

Hage, Ghassan. 2016. État de siège: A Dying Domesticatin Colonialism? *American Ethnologist* 43 (1): 38–49.

Holmes, Seth M., and Heidi Castañeda. 2016. Representing the "European refugee Crisis" in Germany and Beyond: Deservingness and Difference, Life and Death. *American Ethnologist* 43(1): 12–24.

Hudson, Valerie M. 2016. Europe's Man Problem: Migrants to Europe Skew Heavily Male—And That's Dangerous. *Politico*, January 5. Available at: https://www.politico.com/magazine/story/2016/01/europe-refugees-migrant-crisis-men-213500.

Hudson, Valerie M., and Andrea M. Den Boer. 2005. *Bare Branches: The Security Implications of Asia's Surplus Male Population*. Cambridge: MIT Press.

Kenyon Lischer, Sarah. 2017. The Global Refugee Crisis: Regional Destabilization & Humanitarian Protection. *Daedalus* 146 (4): 85–97.

Khader, Bichara. 2016. Muslims in Europe: The Construction of a 'Problem'. In *The Search for Europe: Contrasting Approaches*, ed. F. González, 303–324. BBVA: Open Mind Project.

Kirka, Danica. 2015. *Tip of the Iceberg: No End in Sight to Migrant Wave*. Associated Press, October 4. Available at: https://www.chicagotribune.com/nation-world/sns-bc-eu–migrants-endless-wave-20151004-story.html.

Klaus, Witold. 2020. Between Closing Borders to Refugees and Welcoming Ukrainian Workers: Polish Migration Law at the Crossroads. In *Europe and the Refugee Response. A Crisis of Values?*, ed. Elżbieta M. Goździak, Izabella Main, and Brigitte Suter, 74–90. London: Routledge.

Koening, Matthias. 2005. Incorporating Muslim Migrants in Western Nation States: A Comparison of the United Kingdom, France and Germany. *Journal of International Migration and Integration* 6 (2): 219–234.

Koselleck, Reinhart. 2006. Crisis. *Journal of the History of Ideas* 67 (2): 357–400.

Kurz, Sebastian. 2017. Only by Regaining Control Can We Solve the Migration and Refugee Crisis. *Time*, December 18. Available at: http://time.com/5068561/sebastian-kurz-austria-chancellormigrant-crisis/.

McMahon, Simon, and Nando Sigona. 2018. Navigating the Central Mediterranean in a Time of "Crisis": Disentangling Migration Governance and Migrant Journeys. *Sociology* (3): 497–514.

Migrációkutató Intézet. 2016. Közvéleménykutatás-sorozat a migráció társadalmi megítéléséről V. [Survey series on the social opinion about migration V.].

Miller, Barbara D. 2001. Female-Selective Abortion in Asia: Patterns, Policies, and Debates. *American Anthropologist* 103 (4): 1083–1095. https://doi.org/10.1525/aa.2001.103.4.1083.

Noack, Rick. 2016. Leaked Document Says 2,000 Men Allegedly Assaulted 1,200 German Women on New Year's Eve. *The Washington Post*, July 11. Available at: https://www.washingtonpost.com/news/worldviews/wp/2016/07/10/leaked-document-says-2000-men-allegedly-assaulted-1200-german-women-on-new-years-eve/.

Pędziwiatr, Konrad. 2015. Islamophobia in Poland 2015 Report. In *European Islamophobia Report*, ed. E. Bayrakli and F. Hafez, 425–441. Istanbul: SETA.

Pickel, Gert. 2018. Perceptions of Plurality: The Impact of the Refugee Crisis on the Interpretation of Religious Pluralization in Europe. In *Religion in the European Refugee Crisis*, ed. U. Schmiedel and G. Smith, 15–38. Cham: Palgrave Macmillan.

Simon, László L. 2015. Szaporodjunk! Népszabadság Online, September 5. Available at: http://nol.hu/video/lsimon-a-szaporodasban-latja-a-jovot-1573295.

Sohlberg, Jacob, Peter Esaiasson, and Johan Martinsson. 2019. The Changing Political Impact of Compassion Evoking Pictures: The Case of the Drowned

Toddler Alan Kurdi. *Journal of Ethnic and Migration Studies* 45 (13): 2275–2288. https://doi.org/10.1080/1369183X.2018.1538773.

Squires, Nick. 2019. UN Urges Europe to Allow 500 Migrants Stranded on Rescue Boats to be Allowed to Come Ashore. *The Telegraph*, August 13. Available at: https://www.telegraph.co.uk/news/2019/08/13/un-urges-europe-allow-500-migrants-stranded-rescue-boats-allowed/.

Terrio, Susan J. 2006. Who Are the Rioters in France? *Anthropology News*, January.

Than, Krisztina. 2018. Hungary Could Pass 'Stop Soros' Law Within a Month After Re-Electing Viktor Orban's Anti-Immigrant Government. *The Independent*, 9 April. Available at: https://www.independent.co.uk/news/world/europe/hungary-viktor-orban-ngo-ban-migration-security-risk-george-soros-ban-a8295731.html.

Wike, Richard, Bruce Stokes, and Katie Simmons. 2016. *Europeans Fear Wave of Refugees Will Mean More Terrorism, Fewer Jobs*. Washington, DC: Pew Research Center for the People & the Press. Available at: https://www.pewresearch.org/global/2016/07/11/europeans-fear-wave-of-refugees-will-mean-more-terrorism-fewer-jobs/.

Zunes, Stephen. 2017. Europe's Refugee Crisis, Terrorism, and Islamophobia. *Peace Review: a Journal of Social Justice* 29: 1–6.

CHAPTER 8

Conclusions: Way Forward

Dear Reader,

By now you have read several chapters debating the relationship between security and human trafficking, and, more broadly, international migration. As you have seen, the debates are fervent, but the empirical evidence linking human trafficking and international migration to organized crime and security risks is scarce.

Trafficking in persons is often portrayed as the world's fastest growing criminal enterprise, with profits that rival the illegal drugs and arms trade. Reports repeatedly quote the number of seven billion dollars in profit to indicate the magnitude of the phenomenon (Spangenberg 2002; Denisova 2001; Scarpa 2006; Roby 2005). Reports also talk about networks of international organized crime which are attracted to the trade in human beings because of low risk and because the criminal penalties for human trafficking are light in most countries (Pochagina 2007; Tiefenbrun 2002; Zhang et al. 2007). Media and international organizations also talk about the fact that the crime of trafficking in persons offers international organized crime syndicates a low-risk opportunity to make billions of profits by taking advantage of unlimited supply and unending demand for trafficked persons (Claramunt 2002; Burke et al. 2005).

As I wrote at the outset, numerous authors focus on the alleged connections between sophisticated, organized crime networks and human trafficking, often repeating arguments developed in an empirical vacuum

E. M. Goździak, *Human Trafficking as a New (In)Security Threat*,
https://doi.org/10.1007/978-3-030-62873-4_8

by law enforcement agencies (see Salt 2000; Bruckert and Parent 2002 for more detailed discussion). There are also scholars who contest "the trafficking-as-organized crime thesis" (Lee 2011: 90).

It is not my intention to side with one or the other camp; it is difficult to support the different positions without robust empirical research. It is tempting to see human trafficking as a phenomenon dominated and controlled by organized crime and see the criminal networks as a threat to national security. As a criminal activity, human trafficking is not only an affront to human rights and dignity; it also raises security concerns. Some forms of trafficking—sexual exploitation, forced marriage, and forced labor—are particularly prevalent in the context of armed conflict.

Jamille Bigio and Rachel B. Vogelstein (2019) argue that human trafficking can fuel conflict by enabling armed and extremist groups to raise income and expand their power and military capabilities. The authors invoke the self-proclaimed Islamic State in Iraq and Syria and Boko Haram in Nigeria who have apparently generated considerable revenue from sex trafficking. They argue that governments may profit as well since state-sponsored trafficking can provide corrupt regimes a source of income and bolster their military capabilities. Furthermore, human trafficking can also drive displacement and destabilize communities, thereby exacerbating conflict and undermining development. These are all very logical arguments, but we need empirical proof. There is some evidence that security forces and peacekeepers are unfortunately too often part of the problem in contexts of human trafficking in conflict zones (see Hoang 2019; Mendelson 2005). When committed by security forces and peacekeepers, human trafficking undercuts the ability of international institutions to carry out their missions of promoting peace and stability.

But are traffickers always or predominantly associated with large criminal networks? More importantly, is their goal to undermine national or local security? In reality, the picture is quite complex (Williams 2008). In my own research with trafficked adolescent and young adult women, I have not uncovered any involvement of criminal networks in the trafficking of foreign-born youth into the United States. The vast majority of the youth I studied were smuggled or, in some instances, brought to the United States legally across the US-Mexico border and through different airports. The vast majority of the 'traffickers' that facilitated the journey of the young people were their parents, grandparents, neighbors, and boyfriends. Although in many cases the journey of these young people started as a smuggling operation, it ended—at least in the eyes of the law, if not in the eyes of the youth—in exploitation or abuse. Law enforcement considered working children to be exploited and abused, often without considering the conditions under which the youngsters worked. Therefore, the girls and boys were deemed to be victims of trafficking and their relatives were tried in courts of law on charges of child trafficking. "The Pied Piper who leads the children away with their parents' blessing is the key to this modern slavery," the journalist James Astill states. "Often one of the child's own relatives, he is commissioned to take full advantage of the extended family, and of the poor man's assumption that anywhere is better than here" (Astill 2001).

Smaller operations based on kinship or friendship ties may, of course, be part of larger criminal networks. In my research, however, I have not uncovered any direct evidence of such connections. Moreover, the trafficked girls did not speak of criminal networks, but rather focused on the close relationships between themselves and those who helped them cross the US border and find employment. "This is my mother," cried Isa, one of the young women 'rescued' from a bar where she worked, "where are you taking her?" Despite this reality, policy-makers, child advocates, and service providers maintained a studied blindness toward the complicated role family and kin play in facilitating and financing the migration journeys of children and adolescents to the United States (Goździak 2016).

The US anti-trafficking law treats minors under the age of eighteen as having no volition and therefore as being unable to consent to being smuggled. The law does not embrace the principle of the "evolving capacities" of the child introduced in the 1989 Convention on the Rights of the Child. This principle recognizes that as children acquire enhanced competencies there is a diminishing need for protection and a greater capacity to take responsibility for decisions affecting their lives. The Convention allows for the recognition that minors in different environments and cultures, and faced with diverse life experiences, will acquire competencies at different ages. Under the TVPA of 2000, minors—even those on the verge of adulthood, and who may no longer identify as children—are always trafficked, never smuggled, and those who help them are always traffickers, never just parents, uncles, or family friends trying to give them a better life.

When I taught in Istanbul in 2017, my students included several Syrian refugees. During a lecture on human trafficking, I asked them if they had been trafficked or knew someone who had. They answered with a resounding "No" and proceeded to tell me how they or their families secured the assistance of smugglers to get them over to Turkey. Family members and friends helped them identify smugglers who successfully made the journey from Syria to Turkey. They also talked about family members and friends who hired boat owners to get them to Greece. The refugees did not minimize the difficulties and the dangers involved in the smuggling operations. However, they did not identify as trafficked victims. One young man shared his story with a local NGO helping refugees and was told to narrate his experiences as trafficking. The young man was 17 years old when he came over to Turkey. The smuggler charged him more than originally agreed upon and the journey took longer than anticipated; the NGO staff operationalized it as fraud, one of the elements in the definition of human trafficking. Adding his status as a minor, they were convinced that his flight in search of security [*sic*!] constituted trafficking.

We also chatted about security concerns expressed by policy-makers in Europe and beyond. The Young men were aware that many policy-makers and some members of different European societies consider them a security risk. They pointed out, however, that they fled armed conflict, mandatory conscription, and lack of security in Syria. They stressed that they did not intend to cause trouble of any sort, all they wanted was some stability in their young lives, access to education, and a prospect for decent livelihoods.

These examples show that smuggling is often conflated with human trafficking. Granted, the distinction between trafficking and smuggling is not always easy to make. Lack of robust participatory research with migrants limits our understanding of how migrants perceive those who facilitate their migration journeys. Do they see them as traffickers, smugglers, or simply as hired hands? Although many reports indicate involvement of large criminal networks in human trafficking, family involvement in trafficking should not be underestimated. Are these smaller kinship-based operations part of larger criminal networks? At the moment, we have no tangible proof, mainly suppositions.

In the early 2000s, several scholars bemoaned the fact that the dominant anti-trafficking discourse is not evidence-based but grounded in the construction of particular mythology of trafficking (Sanghera 2005). "With few empirical studies available, imagination seems to have filled the gaps in our knowledge," wrote Sheldon X. Zhang (2009: 1978). "*In no area* of the social sciences has ideology contaminated knowledge more pervasively than in writings on the sex industry," asserted Ronald Weitzer, a sociologist at the George Washington University. This claim certainly extends to trafficking for sexual exploitation, an area "where cannons of scientific inquiry are suspended and research deliberately skewed to serve a particular political [and moral] agenda (Weitzer 2005: 934; see also Weitzer 2007"). Almost two decades later, the situation has not changed much.

What is the way forward? Every sovereign state has a right to ensure national security. Many states do it through foreign policy efforts, border control, immigration admission policies, and a myriad of other provisions allowing or disallowing certain foreign-born people to settle and work in their territories. States have the right to do this, in my opinion. They also have the right to set up a vetting process to evaluate who is a *bona fide* refugee or asylum seeker. However, states should not assume that migrants, refugees, and asylum seekers of certain ethnicity or creed constitute a threat to national security of the countries where they seek refugee or better economic opportunities. There is also a need for a paradigm shift in local communities to ensure that refugees and asylum seekers are not othered and seen as a threat to the social cohesion of local communities.

The attempts to protect state security and sovereignty have to go hand-in-hand with efforts to ensure human security of both hosts and newcomers. The concept of security needs to be broadened. The focus needs to be deepened from nation-state (national security) to people (human security). There needs to be a recognition of the existence of threats from within and outside of the state. I write this fully cognizant that the concept of 'human security' has been contested and that "even some of the strongest proponents of human security recognize that it is at best poorly defined and unmeasured, and at worst a vague and logically inconsistent slogan" (King and Murray 2001: 591). However, switching "the referent from the state to individuals and shifting the focus from military threats to the state to political, eco- nomic, environmental, and gender-based threats to individuals" (MacFarlane and Khong 2006: 237) can be beneficial when it is used as a vehicle to help garner resources and attention from policy-makers for unconventional security issues (see Aradau 2004), including the well-being of refugees and asylum seekers who fled both national and human insecurity resulting from armed conflicts.

And finally, I also want to call for an evidence-based approach to the policies at the nexus of security and human trafficking. There is a need to support robust and independent basic and applied research testing the hypothesis that human trafficking threatens security of whole countries and communities. There is also a need to involve victims of trafficking, refugees, asylum seekers, and labor migrants in the design and execution of well-thought-out studies. It is not enough to invite them as advisors, they must be equal partners as co-researchers.

References

Aradau, Claudia. 2004. The Perverse Politics of Four-Letter Words: Risk and Pity in the Securitization of Human Trafficking. *Millennium: Journal of International Studies* 33 (2): 251–277.

Astill, James. 2001. The Terrible Truth About the Ship of Slaves. *The Guardian*, April 21.

Bigio, Jamille, and Rachel B. Vogelstein. 2019. *The Security Implications of Human Trafficking*. Council on Foreign Relations report. Available at: https://cdn.cfr.org/sites/default/files/report_pdf/Discussion_Paper_Bigio_Vogelstein_Security_Trafficking_OR.pdf.

Bruckert, Christine, and Collette Parent. 2002. *Trafficking in Human Beings and Organized Crime: A Literature Review*. Ottawa: Research and Evaluation Branch, Canadian Mounted Police.

Burke, Alicia, Stafania Ducci, and Giuseppina Maddaluno. 2005. *Trafficking in Minors for Commercial Sexual Exploitation: Costa Rica*. Torino, Italy: UNICRI.

Claramunt, Maria Cecilia. 2002. *Commercial Sexual Exploitation of Minors: Costa Rica*. Geneva, Switzerland: International Labor Organization.

Denisova, Tatiana A. 2001. Trafficking in Women and Children for Purposes of Sexual Exploitation: The Criminological Aspect. *Trends in Organized Crime* 6 (3/4): 30–36.

Goździak, Elżbieta M. 2016. *Trafficked Children and Youth in the United States: Reimagining Survivors*. New Brunswick: Rutgers University Press.

Hoang, Thi. 2019. When the Peacekeepers Are Part of the Problem. Available at: https://globalinitiative.net/when-the-peacekeepers-are-part-of-the-problem/.

King, Gary, and Christopher Murray. 2001. Rethinking Human Security. *Political Science Quarterly* 116 (4): 585–610.

Lee, Maggie. 2011. *Trafficking and Global Crime Control*. London: Sage.

Macfarlane, Neil, and Yuen Foong Khong. 2006. *Human Security and the UN: A Critical History*. Bloomington, IN: Indiana University Press.

Mendelson, Sarah E. 2005. *Peacekeepers and Human Trafficking in the Balkans*. Washington, DC: Center for Strategic and International Studies.

Pochagina, Olga. 2007. Trafficking in Women and Children in Present-Day China. *Far Eastern Affairs* 35 (1): 82–101.

Roby, Jini L. 2005. Women and Children in the Global Sex Trade: Toward More Effective Policy. *International Social Work* 48 (2): 136–147.

Salt, John. 2000. Trafficking and Human Smuggling: A European Perspective. *International Migration* 38 (3): 31–56.

Sanghera, Jyoti. 2005. Unpacking the Trafficking Discourse. In *Trafficking and Prostitution Reconsidered: New Perspectives on Migration, Sex Work and Human Rights*, ed. Kamala Kempadoo, 3–24. Boulder: Paradigm Publishers.

Scarpa, Silvia. 2006. Child Trafficking: International Instruments to Protect the Most Vulnerable Victims. *Family Court Review* 44 (3): 429–447.

Spangenberg, Mia. 2002. International Trafficking of Children to New York City for Sexual Purposes. Available at: https://opencuny.org/childrenincrisis/files/2014/01/Spangenberg-2002-International-Trafficking-of-Children-to-New-York-City-for-Sexual-Purposes.pdf<br.

Tiefenbrun, Susan W. 2002. Sex Sells But Drugs Don't Talk: Trafficking of Women Sex Workers and an Economic Solution. *Thomas Jefferson Law Review* 24: 161–189.

US TIP. Trafficking in Persons. Reports 2003–2020. Available at: https://www.state.gov/wp-content/uploads/2020/06/2020-TIP-Report-Complete-062420-FINAL.pdf.

Weitzer, Ronald. 2005. Flawed Theory and Method in Studies of Prostitution. *Violence Against Women* 11 (7): 934–949.

Weitzer, Ronald. 2007. The Social Construction of Sex Trafficking: Ideology and Institutionalization of a Moral Crusade. *Politics and Society* 35 (3): 447–475.

Williams, Phil. 2008. Trafficking in Women: The Role of Transnational Organized Crime. In *Trafficking in Humans: Social, Cultural and Political Dimensions*, ed. Sally Cameron and Edward Newman. Tokyo: United Nations University Press.

Zhang, Sheldon X. 2009. Beyond the 'Natasha' Story—A Review and Critique of Current Research on Sex Trafficking. *Global Crime* 10 (3): 178–195.

Zhang, Sheldon X., Ko-Lin Chin, and Jody Miller. 2007. Women's Participation in Chinese Transnational Human Smuggling: A Gendered Market Perspective. *Criminology* 54 (3): 699–733.

Index

E. M. Goździak, *Human Trafficking as a New (In)Security Threat*,
https://doi.org/10.1007/978-3-030-62873-4

The manufacturer's authorised representative in the EU is Springer Nature Customer Service Centre GmbH, Europaplatz 3, 69115 Heidelberg, Germany. If you have any concerns regarding our products, please contact ProductSafety@springernature.com

Printed and bound by CPI Group (UK) Ltd, Croydon, CR0 4YY
30/09/2026
02225475-0012